Poets

I0086729

A play

by James Murphy

Published by The Heretic's Press
London
www.hereticspress.co.uk

Front & back cover photo showing a detail from
'Flaming June'
by Frederick, Lord Leighton
courtesy of Heretics Press
Front and back cover design
by Chris Derrick @www.unauthorizedmedia.com

Poets

Published by The Heretic's Press
London
www.hereticspress.co.uk

By the same author

To Hell in a Handcart (play script)
Stroke (play script)
Crash the Bus (novel)
The art of Exile (poetry)
The Misanthropist's Secret Love Life (poetry)
Handbook for the Damned (cultural & literary criticism)

ISBN 978-1-9996149-1-1

© *2018*
The Heretic's Press
www.hereticspress.co.uk

Poets

'For what is human happiness, gentlemen –
nay, heaven itself,
if not living and learning,
laughing and lamenting
with those we love…'

…but one lie
can change everything…

A scandalous reinvention
of
The Shelley-Byron romantic myth…

Born in 1957, James Murphy grew up in the suburbs of South London. He graduated in Philosophy from the University of East Anglia at Norwich. He then worked in several different fields (sometimes literally), including journalism and teaching. During the 1980s, he lived in Tuscany. He recently moved to Sussex, his house having burned down in Hampshire (as per Nietzsche's metaphorical Vesuvian exhortation). He is married with a son.

By the same author

Crash the Bus (novel)
To Hell in a Handcart (play-script)
Stroke (play script)
The Misanthropist's Secret Love Life (poetry)
The art of Exile (poetry)
Wrongdoing (poetry)
Handbook for the Damned (cultural & literary criticism)

LEAVING LIGURIA

Crossing the French border,
Already we have lost the Quattrocento light.
Dusk is sepulchral; the sun, ancestral:
Suddenly sunset's cortege of colours
Bears funereal thoughts in train.

Italy! Land of heat-haze and half-lit truths!
Dawns of silent snow and castellated shadow!
Barely habitable rooms thronged with ancestors!
Sequestered valleys, villages lost in siesta,
Empty afternoons! Whole seasons of loneliness!

Italy! If memories are passageways to the dead,
Embalm the moods that die with our departure!
Haunt the chambers of imagination's catacombs!
Shine a flaming torch within the dull hereafter!
Illuminate the darkness of our sunless Northern tombs!

James Murphy © 2018 The Heretic's Press

Poets

A play by

James Murphy

That summer....

If youth is a time for a kind of holy recklessness; for pursuing rebellious ideals without compromise or prior thought for one's own or anyone else's psychological or physical safety; then the summer of 1819, when Lord Byron, Percy Shelley, Mary Shelley, her half-sister, Claire Claremont and other friends joined forces in Pisa ('collided' might be a better word), must constitute an archetypal moment in the history of youthful Romanticism.

For Romanticism was, quintessentially, a youthful movement. The 'old world' was dying on its feet; its moribund, monarchist, conservative, political, moral and spiritual systems, were ripe for revolution, as young firebrands (and some old ones!) perceived them. America in 1776 and France in 1789 had already broken free from the tyranny of the 'ancien regime'; now democracy – that old Greek illusion – would be the phoenix that would flare up from its ashes with a splendour hitherto unseen. Thus, across Europe, 'free spirits' of varying levels of genius and species of conviction threw themselves with all the bravura at their disposal against the violently repressive forces of the age. That they did so at the cost of their illusions and, in some cases, their lives, has, of course, only served to confirm the glory of Romanticism's archetypal heroes.

As poets, Byron's and Shelley's own roles in this cultural upheaval would be played out in the spheres of philosophy, aesthetics and moral principles rather than in any specifically political realm. In a very real sense - and prefiguring the major players of every successive cultural (as distinct from political) insurrection thereafter, the 1960s included – *Byron's and Shelley's revolution was ultimately who they were*: individuals driven by aesthetic temperaments to lead life-styles that suited their ideals. By actually living out their new moral codes together they advertised a new way of living applicable to, and practicable by, anyone who so chose...presumably whether artistically gifted or not – though having a private income certainly helped!

I

Indeed, this same, necessarily vague ideal had been envisaged by Coleridge, Wordsworth and Southey a generation earlier, with their idea for 'Pantisocracy', or government by all according to principles held in common by all, to be realised in a new community in America. That the latter never ultimately materialised did not diminish its desirability where the next generation was concerned.

Indeed, as with all ideals, it was important not to think about them too deeply in advance, not to dim their theoretical splendour with any pedantic, practical consideration of the respective talents of the people involved in executing them, burdened as they all were with their various predispositions and emotional prejudices – weighed down, so to speak, with all their inevitable 19th century psychological baggage!

Of course, as with every attempt at communal living throughout history (an idea as old as some very old stone age hills!), where the success of the venture is concerned, the devil is in the detail – and all too often the devil in this particular case was Byron.

As events transpired, the so-called 'Pisan circle' that formed along the Lungarno that summer in 1819 proved to be not so much a unified band of expatriate friends as a volatile arena in which impassioned individuals of extraordinary talent struggled over their ideals and philosophies and fought for possession of their own (and each other's) lovers, children and homes. Not that any of this could really have been avoided. The spirit of the age revelled, as aforementioned, in the Dionysian spirit of destruction and renewal. Moreover, given the highly-strung personalities involved, it was no doubt inevitable it should all ultimately end in tears.

Ultimately, Lord Byron and Percy Shelley, became disenchanted and disgusted with each other. But not before they had profoundly influenced each other's lives and deaths and all of those closest to them. Indeed, the poets' very deaths, within two years of each other – Shelley's in a storm-tossed boat, Byron's in war-struck Greece - ultimately occurred as a direct result of the failure of plans they had conceived together. Thus, as a paradigm of the dangers of Romanticism

II

in general and the failure of friendship in particular, their lives became a kind of living poem, a poetic testament to their beliefs.

But why retell the Romantic myth? Do its values really still possess any relevance to our current moral, political and spiritual dichotomies and dilemmas? In an age of hard-bitten urban truths isn't the Shelley-Byron story simply psychological old hat, fit only to be consigned to the metaphorical and actual dressing up box of fusty, musty costume drama?

In vigorously opposing such a view – and refuting the ideological obsession of our myopic history-phobic age - we would argue that it is in the nature of great myths to embody eternal truths. Moreover, that the timeless myth of the young hero and the challenge confronting him - namely, how to foster one's own individual humanity in the face of a corrupt body politic and a decadent spiritual authority - remains as relevant today as they were in Byron's and Shelley's age. Indeed, the Romantics can accurately be seen as prototype Moderns. In this sense, then, we owe it to ourselves to learn from the experiences of the great hearts and minds of the past.

That said, we are happy to concede that, to keep its flame alive and to keep its heart beating in the breast of contemporary culture, every great myth needs reinterpreting from age to age. For this reason *Poets* re-invents the Shelley-Byron legend; indeed, retells its story with some scandalous new twists and turns.

Admittedly, as an historical document *Poets* is wildly unreliable; shamelessly replete, as it is, with vivid half-truths and dramatic conjectures. Indeed, alternating moments of acerbic comedy with bleak nihilism, *Poets'* inflammatory plot incendiarises the tinder-dry facts of history. Not so much a play about Romanticism as an evocation of it. *Poets* ruthlessly sacrifices historical detail in the name of imaginative truth. Furthermore, in being faithless with the facts the play aims to be true to a deeper, more powerful and poetic reality. Thus, in *Poets* Shelley attacks not only religion (he was famously expelled from Oxford for his atheism), but also confronts an Abbess in an Italian

III

priory; he also accidentally contributes to the eventual death of his friend, Lord Byron. Likewise, Shelley's wife, Mary, in real life highly suspicious of Byron's motives and manners, goes one step further in *Poets* and confronts him in a romantically and erotically charged encounter.

Refashioned thus, *Poet's* plot gives new voice to eternal questions; to wit: is idealism a sickness or a cure? Can humanism and religion ever really co-exist? Is God an illusory tyrant or a real redeemer? Is love compatible with romance? How much, if anything, should we sacrifice in the pursuit of truth in human relationships?

In writing Poets, then, it has been our growing conviction that, contrary to the old cliché, *life is not stranger than fiction, but does, itself, constitute the essence of fiction.* Myths work precisely because they reveal our deeper truths. If we were to delve amongst the best and most dramatic elements of our own personal histories we would discover that they, too, reveal hidden patterns and archetypal narratives; even, perhaps, possess a mythical quality. In this context, in weaving together the various strands of the stories of these extraordinary young people's lives, we have simply sought to unify the themes of Romanticism into one coherent dramatic plot.

And then again, of course, when all is said and done, there remains the simple undeniable fact that the Shelley-Byron myth will always be one hell of a story...

James Murphy. South Downs, Hampshire, Summer 2018

Poets – Cast (and notes)

BYRON – Poet, early 30s, the darling of a society he hates. A man of conspicuously unreconciled opposites: romantic/cynic; ecstatic/lethargic; elitist/vulgar; gay/straight; gregarious/misanthropic – all things to all men and nothing to anyone. Friend of Shelley.

SHELLEY – Poet, late 20s, an iconoclast, sees a truth and immediately wonders if it's breakable. Pursues the logic of his inclinations heedlessly. A natural lover of women, prone to being profoundly, alarmingly unromantic. Friend to the above.

MARY SHELLEY – Novelist, early 20s, a young woman of steely intellectual independence, tempered by a romantic disposition which she almost resents in herself. Wife to Shelley, half-sister to the below.

CLAIRE CLAREMONT – Unadulterated romantic, early 20s, contemptuous of anyone lacking the gift of spontaneity. Vibrant and vivacious, she demands only that no-one should make any demands of her. Former lover to Byron and mother of a child he resentfully recognises as his.

FLETCHER – Byron's manservant, early 50s, faithful to a fault, disguises his wisdom behind a veil of slow-wittedness. A patient man, he is slow to rise to any bait offered, but also slow to let it go once grasped.

TRELAWNEY - An adventurer, early 30s, a statue of a man, happily anti-intellectual, he nevertheless possesses a sharp mind which he uses to cut perceived pomposity in others down to size. Great friend to Shelley and a qualified admirer of Byron.

ABBESS dell'ADUMBRINA – An Abbess, mid 50s. English by birth, but called to the church in Italy, she commands the local Abbey. Possessing both vigour and purpose, she is nevertheless an anxious woman aware of the passing of the great age of the church, but determined to do all she can to arrest its decline.

HAYDEN – An accomplished painter, late 20s, earnest, perceives a sense of humour as a decadent luxury that the serious artist should do without. Nevertheless begrudgingly allows it in Shelley and Byron. Romantically attracted to Claire.

ELISE – French-Swiss, mid 20s, a nanny to Claire's baby daughter, and factotum to Mary. Member of the Shelley household, resentful of her status as employee.

POLIDORI – Friend and personal doctor to Byron. Early 30s, an opportunistic, gay-spirited, rootless drifter - charm is his key to entry to the poets' circle.

HUNT - Member of the poets' circle of friends, and an author of renown in his own right, he mistakenly regards himself as their equal. Early 30s.

An Italian strumpet - Early 20s, volatile, voluble lover to Byron.

An Italian manservant – Early 30s, sly, lazy, four or five important lines.

Two young nuns, Sister Paola, Francesca, (strategically important with several lines each).

An Italian osteria landlord.

5 or 6 Dinner guests - (strategically important parts each with single lines.)

Production notes

The play takes place over four acts, shifting scene from London in the first, to the Ligurian coast in north-west Italy for the rest.

Staging should be simple with minimum clutter. Lighting design is key in recreating the contrast of moods between London and the Mediterranean and the brilliantly adumbrated varieties of the latter.

Note re: sound and music

Throughout the play, soft acoustic guitar music of varying moods may be chosen to link the scenes.

Sound effects of rain, waves and thunder, and, at night-time, Italian crickets are required.

VIII

Act 1. sc 1

London. An early evening in late summer. A dimly lit drawing-room suffused with soft sunset light via a window. A figure, Byron's, is seen shifting to and fro, dodging a punch-bag whilst delivering combination punches and talking to himself.

BYR: The trick … is never to stand still! Never to let the other man or woman – lay a hand on you. Outwit your opponent in the mind…and the body will follow. The secret… is never to get within arm's length - of anyone…

Enter Fletcher armed with walking-stick. Byron lays off punch-bag.

FLE: Who's there?!

BYR: Me, you fool – who else were you expecting?

FLE: I didn't think you was due back yet, milord.

BYR: That accounts for the state of the room. Well? Is it ready?

FLE: Cook's got everything in hand.

BYR: The Claret?

FLE: Uncorked and breathing gently like a young maid dreaming, milord.

BYR: Very bucolic, I'm sure.

FLE: Should be, it's the strongest in the cellar.

BYR: Such wit - and from one so poorly paid.

1

Fletcher opens curtains.

[Byron cont.]

Leave those curtains man - I haven't slept for two nights and you scourge me with sunlight!

FLE: Plenty more where that came from in Italy, milord.

BYR: If I go, Fletcher...if I go. Hold this!

Fletcher grasps the punch-bag. Byron begins peppering it with punches. Fletcher, beleaguered, puffs and groans.

Madness to agree to it: living in a papist madhouse with a bunch of half-wits and atheists!

FLE: *I* believe in god, sir.

BYR: --And I'm sure god is very grateful, Fletcher! I'm talking about Shelley, you idiot: not enough for him to bore his friends to death with his beliefs - fool has to spread his atheistic gospel to every damned stranger he meets! The new freethinking philosophy! *(fills wine glass, downs it imperiously, then returns to peppering the punch-bag)* - Man is no longer redeemed by god but damned by him; no more the happy servant but the humiliated slave; a creature not fallen but pushed, as it were, from above! Yes, they'll love that in the Vatican! Truth's fool, that's Shelley. Unfortunately, there is still the child to consider - god, how I hate children. Yes, they're all very sweet and charming - as long as you can give them back to their mothers after thirty seconds of dandling - the idea of living with them!

FLE: Now milord's talking nonsense: you know he is: milord's as good a father as any young lady could wish for - when he's there. As for Miss Allegra's mother--

2

BYR: I'm aware of her mother's identity Fletcher! All too aware... *(a wince of pain, he feels his left leg)*

FLE: Shall I get the doctor, milord?

BYR No, no, no. Useless bunch: done me nothing but harm since the day I came into the bloody world *(rubbing leg)* Cretins couldn't even deliver me properly!

FLE: How her ladyship suffered--

BYR: Bugger her ladyship!

FLE: 'Complications at birth'--

BYR: *Life* is a complication that begins at birth, Fletcher, for which death is the only reliable cure. Do you think it's got worse?

FLE: Difficult to say, milord... *(bends down to tend to the offending limb)*

BYR Get off! This is no time for the laying on of hands - especially not ones as grotesque as yours! Well, what are you gawping at? My guests will be here any moment! Fetch my purple waistcoat!

Exit Fletcher. Byron sits, winces again, then drags on his cigar, slowly exhaling the word:

Italy....

Fade.

1.2

Cheap rented rooms across town. Same evening. Clare is seated, reading. Mary paces about, Trelawney leans by a window. Elise darns sullenly. Enter Shelley carrying a bag.

MARY: What time do you call this!

SHEL: Oranges! *(throws Trelawney the bag of oranges, Shelley dons jacket)*

MARY: You promised not to be late: tonight of all nights!

TRE: *(peeling an orange)* One excuse, that's all his Lordship needs!

SHEL: He won't back out now - trust me.

MARY: Why should we? He's a liar and a cheat.

CLA: And a misogynist!

TRE: No wonder women find him irresistible.

SHEL: He'll come because he's dying of boredom - we all are... England's a wasting disease. The cure, however, is at hand: Italia! We'll pluck oranges from the trees and grapes from the vine!

MARY: Clare hates oranges.

CLA: No, I don't.

MARY: And I loathe grapes.

TRE: *(chewing orange gingerly)* God, these *are* bitter--

4

SHEL: *(wryly)* The fruit of matrimony: once tasted nothing remains but a core of indifference. So the ripest passions rot, eh, Mary?

Clock chimes.

MARY: An hour late!

SHEL: Excellent - he'll be furious! Trelawney, the oranges, ladies goodnight! *(he kisses Clare's hand theatrically, then turns to Mary, whose gaze he holds momentarily; exit Shelley and Trelawney. Clare rushes to the window and waves).*

CLA: I wish I were going with them!

MARY: Do you...

CLA: Men always have such fun together! It's a great bore to belong to such a humourless sex!

MARY: Perhaps women don't have as much cause to laugh as men.

CLA: Well, I'd always rather be with men than women – *(Mary demurs)* - not for the reasons you think! Byron's still amusing – even if we can't be civil to each other! Personally I couldn't care less if he never addressed another word to me; in fact, if the villa is as large as he boasts, we shan't have to see each other from one month to the next. But the fact remains, Allegra is his child, she's entitled to benefit from...*(stops herself short)*

MARY: I'm sure Byron will behave with typically 'aristocratic' consideration. They say his wife was treated handsomely enough in the separation, is it not so Elise?

ELISE: That woman – she treated milord like a bank, and expected him to ask nothing in return. She was stupid – like all women who expect something for nothing--

CLA: No, of course - expecting something for nothing is a man's prerogative.

MARY: Then again, sometimes men get more than they bargained for…

Exit Elise. Fade on Mary gazing at fire.

1.3

Byron's billiard-room. Later that evening, In a simultaneous burst of laughter, fire and candle-light illuminate a baize table-top which doubles as a dinner table littered with the aftermath of the meal. The evening has reached the liqueurs and is, in some cases, the worse for wear. An opium pipe is going round.

BYR: It's settled then!

HUNT: *(receiving the opium pipe)* What is?

BYR: The great Italian question, you fool!

HUNT: Really? I must've been out of the room at the time.

TRE: Out of your senses, more like!

Byron begins to wander about.

POLI: Off his head! Out of his brain!

BYR: Oh, you can't blame Hunt for wanting a simple change of scene – I'd go out of my mind if it were as small as his…

6

Byron circumambulates Hunt, knocking on Hunt's head and the table simultaneously

[Byron cont.]

  not enough room for two thoughts at once – are there, Hunt?

HUNT: Not when they're as gross as yours Byron, no.

The sound of general cheering.

  - or as warped as yours!

VOICE: The creature lives!

POLI: Yes, shouldn't a mammal like you be hibernating by now Hunt?

HUNT: I can assure you that if I look somewhat torpid you need look no further than the soporific predictability of the evening's conversation.

POLI: Why – got something against women, have we Hunt?

HUNT: Yes, the fact that you talk about nothing else, Polidori.

BYR: Gentlemen must we continually suffer this bore's insolence?

Jeers in the negative, Byron continues.

You see, Hunt, it appears my guests desire some form of redress for your grievous prudery.

POLI: Yes, haul him up!

VOICE: Put the prig on trial!

Byron takes up his chair and places it upon the table. He then clambers on board the table himself and sits on the chair in judgement. Hunt, now sitting below him is much disconcerted. Shelley observes a wry silence.

HUNT: For god's sake, Byron--

BYR: I, Noel George Gordon, Lord Byron, late of Newstead Abbey, Peer of the Realm, with the power invested in me by His Mad Majesty King George 'Fatty the Fourth' of England, accuse you Leigh Hunt – a commoner if ever there was one – of the unpardonable offence of prudishness in good company! How do you plead?

VOICE: We're not interested in his plea!

HUNT: I wouldn't do you the courtesy of making one.

BYR: And there's further proof of his plebeian arrogance, jurors! I ask all of you to deliver a verdict of guilty without delay!

ALL: Guilty!

BYR: Then I shall deliver the sentence forthwith!

Slowly, Byron begins to tip a carafe of wine on Hunt who rises as the first drops hit him.

HUNT: Stop! For god's sake stop! *(brushing himself)* - The least you can do is give me the chance to choose my own defence!

BYR: My dear fellow, you don't need one – you've been convicted!

HUNT: Then I demand the right of appeal – and I choose the poet Shelley to represent me!

8

BYR: Poet!? We don't want no drivelling poets here, do we lads?
         All that womanly whining annoys us at the best of times.
         Besides which Shelley's barred – he was late for dinner.
         What's more: I've never seen him less drunk: sobriety is a
         great insult to a host, you know, Shelley!

HUNT: But a great quality in an advocate! I demand Shelley be
         allowed to defend me!

BYR: All right, all right! *(he sits in judgement again)* So, Shelley!
         What can you possibly have to say in defence of such an
         idiot?

SHEL: Precisely that.

BYR: What?

SHEL: He's an idiot…. a simpleton.

BYR: Well we won't argue with that will we lads?

HUNT: *(amazed)* Shelley…!

SHEL: And consequently in no position to answer for his actions or
         words! Therefore, I submit it would be improper of any
         court, however nobly constituted, to convict an arrant fool –
         commit him to an asylum, yes - to a common prison, never!

BYR: This is sharp practise Shelley.

SHEL: Necessary to protect a blunt mind, milord!

BYR: But then you must prove his idiocy before we revoke our
         former judgement….it shouldn't be difficult.

SHEL: Indeed not; and if their lordships will allow me to continue I shall, within a matter of moments, cite incontrovertible proof of my client's pathetic stupidity.

BYR: Please, I can hardly bear the lack of suspense.

SHEL: Gentlemen of the jury! We are all saying farewell! Because some of us have the good fortune to be leaving very shortly for Italy, the mere mention of whose name confers upon our melancholic Northern souls honorary citizenship of the antique republic of summer! Italy, gentlemen! – where the sun vigorously exercises his timeless right to shine; where winter, a classical democrat, shares but one season in four and doesn't tyrannously usurp the whole year as in this barbarous gothic clime--

Byron emits audible yawn, so Shelley exclaims in his ear.

Italy! Where the sun is the life and soul of celebration and not, as in our own dismal land, some absent guest of honour whose perennial failure to show his face in June, July and August flattens both the wine and the gaiety of his expectant hosts, suffusing successive British summers with a sober sense of pointlessness. Italy, gentlemen! However…some of us are not so lucky! Some of us are staying behind: vicious circumstance confines them in this damp prison island to which we were all born inmates. Either the unfortunate have no money or, worse still, no imagination. But the fact remains that those to whom the gift of freedom has been granted--

BYR: Are getting the hell out!

Riotous cheering.

SHEL: All, that is, with the sad exception of my poor client. He alone has freely chosen to remain a prisoner here on a spiritual diet of bread and rainwater; even though the door of his cell has been left open by that most capricious gaoler 'fortune!' – for Mr Hunt can most certainly afford to make the journey and he has a wife who, with kind words, could be persuaded to accompany him, yet he will not come; will not come gentlemen, in spite of his knowledge that a palace, courtesy again of Milord - umm - *(cries of "Byron")* - Byron - awaits those of us who make the voyage. A grand palazzo, which, I may add, is destined to promote and protect the constant delight of a company of friends of like minds and hopes. For what is human happiness gentlemen – nay, heaven itself – if not living and learning, laughing and lamenting with those we love?

BYR: What say you Polly, could you learn to love me?

POLI: Byron, I never thought you'd ask.

SHEL: And there you see the spirit and the emblem of our venture gentlemen: a fellowship in hope and aspiration. Now we all know how near allied is genius to madness; imagine then how refulgent with folly must be the mind of my client – a man, mark you, who self-confessedly loves an adventure, but who nevertheless cocks his snook at this, our Italy. The guaranteed romance of its classical past! The unexplored promise of its--

POLI: Women!

SHEL: Future!

Jeers.

VOICE: Puritan!

SHEL: In spite of seas warmer than perfumed baths; of skies bluer than the comeliest maiden's eyes; of meadows softer than feather beds--

VOICE: Better!

SHEL: In spite of fruits more delicious than any god ever forbade--

VOICE: Atheist!

SHEL: In spite of moonlight so bright a man's shadow walks hand-in-hand with him at midnight. In spite of endless summer days that last until Christmas and begin again in January! In spite of festivals whose brilliance blinds the black looks of night and dazzles the dull-witted dawn--

VOICE: More!

SHEL: In spite of all these my client wishes to remain in gaol; wishes indeed to pull firmly shut the door that circumstance has purposely left open. And why, gentlemen? Why? *(Shelley gestures to Byron to stand behind Hunt who, as before, begins to knock on the tabletop at the same time as Hunt's head in time to Shelley's summing up).* Because he is an irremediable, unmitigated, demented, deranged blockhead! Could he be otherwise?

ALL: No! A lunatic! A madman! *(etc)*

SHEL: And therefore I ask that you acquit him!

ALL: Innocent! Innocent!

Applause and general uproar.

BYR: Smart enough defence, I don't deny Shelley – but I think we'll execute the idiot anyway!

Against cries of disapproval Byron makes to pour wine over Hunt, the jeers intensify – 'no for shame', etc.

VOICE: To hell with the aristocracy!

Byron is pelted with orange peel.

HUNT: Yes! Liberty, fraternity and – what's the other one?

BYR: *(accepting his lost cause)* Equality, Hunt – an impossible dream in your case. Fletcher! Set up the billiards! Balls, gentlemen?

Over the following dialogue, the dinner table is cleared and billiards set up.

BYR: Fletcher why ain't there any Bordeaux on the table?

FLE: Because you've drunk it all milord.

BYR: There you see - even my valet moralises at me! And that's why I like him! Because he speaks his mind honestly and I can dismiss him for it if I want! There's no better company than an honest man one doesn't have to listen to: at least one knows one's ignoring the best advice. *(chalks up his cue)* - Come on! Is no-one brave enough to take me on?

VOICE: The painter! He's good with sticks!

Hayden is pushed forward and a cue thrust in hand.

BYR: Yes, come on Hayden, give me a beating – you know you've always wanted to! Tone up the muscles for Italy – who knows you might need' em! *(raises his cue phallically)*

13

HAYD: Is there really any need to be quite so coarse, Byron? –
We're not all going to Italy just to gratify the basest
appetites.

BYR: No, quite right, Hayden: we're going in order to worship at
the Shelleyan shrine of classical knowledge.

HAYD: I didn't say that.

They start to play.

BYR: No you didn't. In fact you didn't say anything. Why are you
coming to Italy, Hayden?

HAYD: I'm going in order to paint, Byron. That's what painters do,
you know: landscapes, portraits--

BYR: Of beautiful women--

HAYD: I shall endeavour to be true to life.

BYR: Ah, yes, the most difficult of arts, Hayden – especially when
it's so much more easy and rewarding to flatter.

HAYD: I flatter myself that a gentleman doesn't need to flatter a
lady.

BYR: Then you do indeed flatter to deceive yourself, my dear
Hayden. What, not use flattery on a woman? You must
never've spoken to one at all or you'd know that merely to
converse with a woman is to have to flatter female sensitivity
to some degree.

HAYD: I don't converse with the subject in the studio Byron, I paint
her.

BYR: Mm. Whether she likes it or not.

14

HAYD: She does like it – in fact, if you must know, women are far more appreciative of art than men.

BYR: And of artists?

HAYD: They are disposed to like those whose paintings they like--

BYR: And those whose paintings are liked are disposed to like those who like their paintings – quite! Well, it's obvious there's no tempting St. Hayden to admit a human side, let alone a love of womankind…

HAYD: That's not true – as it happens, since we're on the subject, and since I was going to mention it earlier--

Roars stilled by Byron's raised hand, the company fall silent.

- there is someone I've had in mind for sometime. However, I intend it to remain a secret.

General groan.

BYR: Indeed, from the poor girl herself, Hayden, if you've as much sympathy for women as you profess--
(to general laughter. Byron speaks the next passage with 'throwaway' speed.) - Anyway, gentlemen, the great Italian question is settled once and for all – some of us are going and some of us are staying. Fact is, we're a simple-hearted bunch: Shelley believes in rainbows with crocks of gold, while the fearlessly penniless Trelawney believes in spending them! Beatific St Hayden here's going to paint every Italian wench he finds a virgin white, whilst Dr Polly Dolly paints their towns red – fat little leech that he is – he knows that no-one else but me would be stupid enough to afford the drain on his finances which his dismal attentions represent.

POLI: Leeches are so expensive these days--

BYR: And life is so cheap! So there you have it: we all have our reasons and we all know what they are, though our letters home shall be reserved strictly to impart the innocent traveller's sense of wonderment – a gorge here, a glacier there; that sort of thing. The important point is that we, as companions know each other's hearts in the matter.

HUNT: Do we? I don't recall hearing your reasons for going Byron.

Cheers.

BYR: Really, Hunt - *(momentarily cold)* - I should've thought my reasons were the most public of all…

Warming up, he begins to perambulate the billiard table.

You obviously haven't been reading the newspaper gossip – oh no, of course, you've been writing it! Well, then you above all should know that I'm going because I no longer have a choice.

TRE: Poor Byron: the prophet despised in his own country—

BYR: Yea, brethren - falsely accused of feats of carnality that would be ludicrous were they not geometrically impossible! Couple this with a demand for divorce from a termagant wife who refuses even to allow him entry… to his own house, and it is surely understandable that the aforementioned reprobate has been driven into warmer waters and the delicious arms of Italian sirens. Game, I think Hayden? Anyway, to hell with marriage! If there's one thing more insufferable than a faithless woman, it's a constant one! Ask Shelley – he may still be married in name – but mentally he's as much a divorcee as I am – eh, Shel? 'Companions of Dishonour' you might call us: hardened veterans of the locked bedroom door,

16

[Byron cont.]

and the distant weeping of damsels in self-imposed distress. But enough of women, gentlemen – the final valedictory toast! I give you all the things we have relished tonight and will doubly do so in the future: to luxury, opium, and – speaking personally – to fame!

All drink and cheer.

POLI: Opiates are a destructive addiction Byron.

TRE: And fame?

SHEL: Worse – it corrodes the conscience.

BYR: How would you know Shelley? Your last atheist polemic only sold four copies--

SHEL: Five, I made Trelawney buy his.

BYR: Another example of fortune's malicious sense of humour: you love the people and they ignore you, whereas I loathe them and they won't leave me alone.

Fletcher renews their drinks.

So, Fletcher! What do you think of Italy?

FLE: It's 'ot, sir.

BYR: And there you have it - no prevarication, no dissembling: in the words of the sage "it's 'ot!" And can a man be happy in Italy, Fletcher?

FLE: Depends whether a man's content to sleep in lousy beds and drink rough wine.

BYR: That's my Fletcher! Always thinking about his belly or his bum! And is there nothing else could entice a man to Italy, Fletcher? What about all the joys my friend Shelley mentioned? The sea? The sky? The moonlight?

FLE: With respect, sir, nothing that can't be had at Brighton, if I may speak my mind, sir?

BYR: Oh speak it, Fletcher, speak it! But there's more to man than that much over-rated organ the mind: what about the other parts of your manhood, Fletcher? That part, for example, that responds to the look in a pretty girl's eyes?

Hayden sighs in exasperation.

FLE: I don't know anything about that, milord.

BYR: Oh come on, Fletcher, you've been casting around for a wife for decades now *(to others)* I'll wager the old codger knows more than all of us! Fletcher, it's your duty as my valet to give us any relevant counsel you may possess!

FLE: Well milord, as I recall from the last time I served you in Italy, the womenfolk--

BYR: Womenfolk, what are they?

FLE: The ladies--

BYR: We don't want to hear about ladies, Fletcher.

FLE: The maidens - *(hesitates as the company sniggers)* - - the maidens are very dark, Milord.

BYR: Dark! Excellent! The maidens are dark! *(beat)* - Where?

FLE: Pardon, milord?

18

BYR: Where are they dark, Fletcher? On their knees? Their
elbows? Their hands? Where?

SHEL: *(laconically)* Spare us, please…

BYR: Spare yourself, Shelley I'm hungry for Fletcher's wisdom.
Dark, Fletcher – where are they dark?

FLE: I'm sure milord's been close enough to see for himself, but if
he really wants my opinion, then I'd say the women was
dark everywhere, but darkest…

Expectant silence.

BYR: Yes, Fletcher…?

FLE: Darkest of all, milord - darkest of all…*(beat)* - in their
hearts.

Roars of approval, glasses raised, etc.

Slow fade.

1.4

*Still Byron's rooms. Later that same evening. Lights up
almost immediately on the party making its adieus,
laughing and leave-takings, etc.*

BYR: Going so soon, Shelley? The night may not be young but it's
still serviceable.

Fletcher helps Shelley & Trelawney with coats.

FLE: You'd do better to retire yourself milord, it's keeping such
odd hours gives you all those nightmares.

BYR: Yes - thank you Fletcher! *(he gestures adieu to Hunt & Hayden)*

FLE: *(to Shelley)* He keeps seeing little Miss Allegra crying her eyes out – then he even dreamt he murdered you last night, sir. No love lost in that dream, I can tell you!

BYR: I said 'thank you' Fletcher!

SHEL: *(ironically)* Our fortunes are bound together – why not our nightmares? More details, Fletcher – who knows what such dreams may mean for us all.

Trelawney shifts uneasily.

Not just for you and me, Byron – Allegra and her future, and her mother too!

BYR: *(irritably)* The girl's mother never comes into my dreams.

SHEL: But you won't deny they concern her daughter.

BYR: Spare me your meditations just for once, Shelley! *(he fills his glass and swigs)* God knows why I allowed myself to be seduced into this preposterous escapade in the first place! You'd do well to remember I merely agreed to set the child up and put a roof over its infernal mother's head! One thing's certain: I haven't escaped the frigid clutches of a noble wife merely to be bound by the shop-girl passions of a sometime mistress. Exactly what atonement would you deem sufficient to expiate one night of dismal pleasure with the damned girl?

TRE: Byron, I hardly think--

BYR: Well do tell me please! I've broken with my wife, I'm contemned in every decent house in London, I'm leaving the

[Byron cont.]

'old' country – good god, I'm even supplying you all with a damned palace in the new one, what more can you possibly want? *(his glass drops and breaks causing an embarrassed silence)* Don't just stand there Fletcher! Fetch another glass!

TRE: Come on Shelley, the heath will take a while.

BYR: The heath? Why in god's name go that way home?

Fletcher returns with a bottle, glass & dustpan.

TRE: Shelley's idea: one last panoramic view of the capital.

BYR: Of course! It'll be spectacular in the pitch dark and rain.

TRE: Actually there's a full moon tonight…. Well, see you on board…

Byron doesn't turn as he replies.

BYR: Oh, I shan't jump ship: god knows why not.

TRE: Goodnight, then – and thanks.

BYR: What for?

Exit Shelley and Trelawney

FLE: Will that be all then, milord?

BYR: *(Stands gazing into the fire).* Yes, Fletcher…sweet dreams.

Fletcher exits sheepishly.

Fade.

1.5

Hampstead Heath. Past midnight, same night. Shelley and Trelawney look out across the audience.

TRE: There: a million souls at rest: humanity in harmony!

SHEL: Principally because they're all asleep.

TRE: *(wryly)* The ideal city!

SHEL: The city of the dead - may they rest in peace, safely stowed in their beds, like bodies in a mausoleum. It's a wonder we *have* such a fear of death when we rehearse it each night so fluently.

Exit Shelley. Trelawney lingers.

TRE: The peace of oblivion. Shame they have to be woken....

Fade.

1.6

Byron's room, curtained. Next day. Chinks of dawn light illuminate a sleeping yet restless Byron slumped in an armchair, empty wine-glass still in one hand. A candelabra gutters on a side-table. Enter Fletcher, in cleaning mode. Byron wakes with a start.

BYR: What time is it?

FLE: It's tomorrow, Milord. Sun'll be breaking through this window any moment – spear you like a chicken it will, if it finds you sitting there; then you'll regret being such a night bird.

BYR: A chicken is not a night bird, Fletcher.... *(he stretches)* Tell me, did I say anything last night that I might live to regret?

FLE: Of course, milord. *(carefully picking up last night's broken wine glasses).*

BYR: Quite. Who cares, anyway! Regrets are like broken glass, Fletcher: fit only for the dust-heap. So - to Italy, eh? Well, I tell you one thing, I'll not live like a damned gypsy with the rest of the troupe. As for the child: we'll see...

Slow fade.

END OF ACT ONE

ACT 2. Sc 1

Italy. A few weeks later in late August. A beech fringed with pines. Hot late-afternoon sun. In the background, a Tuscan song, the sound of breaking waves and noonday cicadas fills the air. An Italian servant crosses the stage, pauses to adjust his burden and continues. Trelawney follows, throws down his own bags, followed by Hayden and Shelley.

TRE: Bloody horses - typical Italian nags! Hell for leather one moment, knackered the next!

HAYD: We shouldn't stop - it's getting late. *(overtakes Trelawney and exits)*

TRE: I'm not moving another step without water! *(calls servant)* - Stop! Signore! – *(to Shelley)* - What the devil's the word for "stop"?

SHEL: Fermati. *(throws down his bags).*

TRE: Ferma - what? God, these bloody cicadas! Can't hear myself think! – Where's the man going now? Couldn't you find anyone better than this dunderhead, Shelley? Fool hasn't a word of English!

SHEL: Shoot him, he's only a peasant.

TRE: Damned if this heat don't drive me to shoot you, too! Unspeakable! Morning, noon and night! What's the point of it! *(kicks sand)* You can't *do* anything in it!

SHEL: I know, isn't it wonderful? *(starts to undress)*.

TRE: What are you doing?

Enter Clare and Mary.

SHEL: Too hot for any labour - but love--

CLA: And poetry...

TRE: And those of us who are neither poets nor lovers?

SHEL: Go naked!

MARY: Why must you always take your clothes off?

SHEL: Why must you always keep yours on? Look around you, Mary: we're free! No more rules or etiquette, no niceties, no pretensions – no clothes! Dance with me!

MARY: Don't be stupid.

CLA: *I* will.

MARY: You'll be caught!

24

CLA: Who by?

MARY: It's against the law.

SHEL: There *are* no laws in paradise.

TRE: Only serpents--

CLA: *(making fun)* And eternal damnation!

SHEL: Let's get her!

MARY: Shelley... Don't you dare! - Trelawney, Clare, you traitor!

Shelley, Trelawney and Clare grab Mary and drag her screaming out into the auditorium sea with exuberant yells. Sounds of the sea and cicadas rise.

2. 2

The villa. Later that evening. An atmosphere of dereliction, furniture is sparse and simple. Trunks, boxes and bags litter the floor. Hayden and Elise unpack. Enter Mary and Clare after first explorations of the house.

CLA: But it's a palace, Mary!

MARY: Yes, an infested one. *(swats insect)* – The mosquitoes!

CLA: *(also swatting)* We'll soon get rid of them; then we'll make it beautiful. Look how this room catches the sunlight!

MARY: It'll be dark soon and you won't see anything. And where are we supposed to sleep without beds! Holes in the ceiling – *(steps to avoid a rotting floorboard)* and the floor! It's preposterous even to consider staying here in these

[Mary cont.]

conditions. Look at these hideous old chests! The whole place looks like a sepulchre strewn with coffins! God knows, if I'd wanted to be sealed alive in a tomb I'd've stayed at home with mother and father!

Enter Byron, followed by Fletcher and Polidori.

BYR: Ladies…

HAYD: About time.

BYR: We're not disturbing you…?

MARY: No, we 're disturbed already.

BYR: *(looking around)* – Hmm, interesting – Shelley not here?

CLA: He went to meet you – you must have missed him.

BYR: Yes, my coachman came by a shortcut I remembered from childhood. Don't worry, Fletcher'll fetch him, he loves an errand – don't you Fletcher.

Exit Fletcher lugubriously.

CLA: Would you like some water - or - anything?

MARY: We would offer you a seat – but there aren't any.

BYR: Yes, it is somewhat Spartan, I agree. 'Swhat comes of trusting sentimental memories of one's childhood! *(he peers about)* Ah, Villa Mare! House of my youth! *(beat)* - What a hole! I swear it's shrunk – this room was enormous last time I stood here! And that trunk! – I used to hide in it with room to spare…!

26

POLI: Yes, when you were six.

BYR: Typical – the agent assured me in his letter the place was still "perfectly appointed" - his very words! 'Spose it is – for a hermit - or some other comfortless soul - Shelley'll love it! *(he gazes out of the windows)* – I told you the beach came up to the house--

POLI: *(emptying out a cupful of sand)* But not into it …

BYR: Shouldn't these windows have glass in them? *(he passes his hands ironically through the frames)* Mmm…palazzo-hunting with a new land-agent next week, eh Polly?

Enter Hayden with a box.

Ah, Hayden, with another box! How useful, in our consummate discomfort…

HAYD: We need to unpack—

BYR: Quite so – I'd help but I'm suffering from chronic dismay brought on by lack of furniture – the only remedy for which, as my good doctor will surely agree, is swift repair to the more humane conditions of the local albergo.

POLI: My diagnosis exactly.

CLA: You're not staying?

BYR: Of course not – and nor will you if you have any sense. Apologies of course, for my childhood...mis-remembrances, but I doubt the creator himself could wrest any form from this particular chaos – I, meanwhile, promise to move heaven and earth next week--

CLA: Next week?

27

BYR: Tomorrow being Sunday, and traditionally my day of rest. Come on Polly! – Oh, send on the fool Fletcher will you?

He exits with a flourish, leaving Polidori to shrug in his wake as he exits himself. Mary angrily pushes aside an old chair as Clare drifts off to another room. Hayden begins to unpack again, tutting at some of the 'useless' things he finds

MARY: For God's sake Hayden – must you?

HAYD: We should still get the place in some sort of order.

Enter Fletcher with bags followed by Shelley and Trelawney.

FLE: What with them round turret things, the whole thing reminds me of the Dome at Brighton, Sir.

SHEL: Home from home eh Fletcher? Where's Byron?

MARY: Where, indeed?

CLA: He's just left.

HAYD: He's going looking for a new palazzo - the furniture and fittings weren't to his liking.

MARY: Nor ours. The noble savage ideal may appeal to you Shelley, but some of us are civilised.

SHEL: A few repairs – what did you expect?

MARY: Tables! Chairs! Beds!

CLA: And there's no running water--

28

MARY: Except through the roof.

SHEL: A tile here and there – a moment's work…

MARY: Well let Byron do it; or have we travelled a thousand miles just to wait on his Lordship!

SHEL: We wait on no-one, Mary - the land, the vines, olive groves – all ours!

MARY: Including the disgusting swamp we crossed to get here!

TRE: Italy wouldn't be Italy without a bit of malaria.

SHEL: One September storm will clear the air, then next year we'll drain--

MARY: Shelley, why do you think all the houses nearby are deserted? The place is unsanitary! Well, you can forget next year, or next week; I'm not staying one night in a filthy, infested, miasmal slum with nowhere to sleep or wash! *(she puts on her shawl and makes to leave)*

CLA: Mary, what are you doing?

MARY: Going to the inn, as your beloved Byron suggested!

CLA: Mary!

Exit Mary followed by Clare remonstrating.

SHEL: Leave her! If she so passionately prefers the infestations of the pensione. *(beat)* Fine community. - Good old Byron…

TRE: One sinking ship – one rat….

SHEL: We're not sunk yet. As for your rat: he can be lured back easily enough. *(moves to window)*

TRE: With what?

SHEL: His appetite for company – and his distaste for solitude.

HAYD: To hell with Byron – we have the ladies to consider.

SHEL: Do we, I don't see any, do you Trelawney?

HAYD: You know full well what I mean.

Hayden throws down a couple of books he's been holding, glares at Shelley and exits. In ironic remonstration Trelawney looks at Shelley who turns back ruefully to the view and the departing figures.

Fade.

2.3

The reception of a modest pensione. Later that afternoon. Byron stands before a desk fronted by a hapless Italian landlord. Byron is unaware of Mary who is sitting silently in the shadows behind him.

BYR: What do you mean, 'full up'?! Where are we – The Champs Elysees?

The landlord shrugs. Byron casts his eyes to the heavens.

Look, I don't wish to pull rank but...*(points to himself)* Lord Byron! – Non ha sentito il mio nome? ... Non conosce come mi chiamo? Do you know who I am?

L'L'D: *(Points behind Byron)* La signora Inglese ha appena preso la scorsa camera! *(to Mary, in broken English)* – Your room ready five minutes – cinque minuti, Signora!

BYR: What English lady? *(turns languidly)* Mary! – You secretive little thing - how long have you been sitting there?

MARY: I didn't like to interrupt: you were in such fine flow.

BYR: Well I hope you're enjoying my hostelry tragedy: all rooms full - looks like the beach for me tonight!

MARY: Oh don't worry, you can have my room; on reflection I think I've just decided not to stay: I've never been stared at so much!

BYR: Some wine – that'll do the trick! Landlord: del vino rosso!

MARY: Not for me.

BYR: Nonsense! You need it! I need it! The world needs it!

MARY: *(a pause, she accepts)* What's the matter with Italians? Haven't they ever seen a foreign woman in a pensione?

BYR: Not alone. It sets them talking. God knows who you might be! A famous French actress? A singer? A woman of ill repute? A young wife in flight from an intellectually over-bearing husband?

MARY: The only thing I'm in flight from is your hideous palazzo – and this heat! Fletcher was right: Italy is the most uncomfortable country I've ever been in!

BYR: I warned Shelley! Told him: Italy's a hell for horses and high-born English ladies! He's led you on, Mary. He

[Byron cont.]

deserves to be punished: leave him - come and live with me -
it'd be scandalous!

MARY: You're incorrigible.

*The landlord reappears with a carafe of wine and two
glasses on a tray, he pours the wine and exits.*

BYR: I hope so: I'd hate to think my vices were mere affectations.
Ah Mary, *(handing a glass to her)* what would it've been
like if I'd met you first!

MARY: *(ironically)* Why, Byron, it would've been just like all your
other love affairs: over in five minutes.

BYR: *(raises his glass to her - they drink)* A successful
relationship, then? At least, in my books.

MARY: Then thank god we don't all read your books.

BYR: Actually you're the only one who doesn't. At least you say
you don't…

MARY: Not true; I said I didn't read them uncritically.

BYR: No, no that's far too many double negatives – do you like
'em or don't you, Mary: be brutal. But be warned: I bear an
implacable grudge.

MARY: I loved Don Juan, as you well know!

BYR: Yes, he is rather irresistible, isn't he?

MARY: Only I don't always think he - or you - do my sex justice.

BYR: I don't *try* to: I write them as I see them - women, I mean.

MARY: But do you always seem them clearly? I sometimes wonder if your experiences in – and out – of love haven't, how shall I put it, blinded you to certain truths.

BYR: Love is blind, Mary, that's what makes its adventures interesting.

MARY: But that's my point: you *see* a woman as a creature only to be loved – or hated. Have you never thought, a woman may not want to be loved; that romance can be an irrelevance for women just as much as men; that she may just want to go about her business - to be treated as a fellow human being.

BYR: How tedious. I'd never do a woman the disservice of treating her like a fellow human being: I have boring friends for that. But you can't fool me, Mary Shelley, this rationalism, this blue-stocking style, it doesn't suit you: every woman wears red. Love is woman's element: she's a bird of prey. We men are flightless birds: you batten on us at will. Don't deny it. I bet you took one look at Shelley across the room and down you swooped!

MARY: I was sixteen--

BYR: The perfect age for swooping! Admit it: he was helpless in your grip. And who can blame you? We're all made for love - predators and prey. We *need* to love and be loved: we can't survive without it. That's why the good lord made us different in the first place: to seek out the ecstasy of union.

MARY: And where does that leave love between men?

BYR: Where it should be: a poor second. Look, the love I feel for Shelley is, well, different from the love I feel for, say, you... and not just love. A woman, any woman, comes into a room and I promise you, any man in that room will immediately respond differently toward her as compared to his comportment with his friends. It's always been so, it must be so. The propagation of the species demands it.

MARY: But must everything be reduced to the animal?

BYR: Indeed not; love liberates the angel in man.

MARY: But not in woman.

BYR: Yes, of course in woman: you misconstrue me on purpose, Mary.

MARY: Still, according to your philosophy, there are no other pursuits men and women may follow?

BYR: Not together. Apart, maybe! A woman may excel in any sphere, just as a man does. But put them together and love always comes between them. Take you and me: I don't deny I treat you as my equal intellectually, and yet, if you were to press me, I'd have to confess that even now my manner, my choice of words, even of thoughts, is amended by my... *(he adjusts her lace sleeve)*... apprehension of your...beauty as a woman.

Mary re-adjusts her sleeve.

I cannot help it. Nor would I wish to. The difference between the sexes is a divine fascination, and overcoming it is a mortal joy. As you'd find out...

MARY: I must go.

BYR: Must you?

MARY: Coming here was stupid - I can't leave Claire--

BYR: But you *can* leave Shelley.

MARY: Percy can look after himself: sometimes I don't think he needs anyone.

BYR: That's what he wants you to think. It's his little game.

MARY: Which he's very good at!

BYR: Indeed! I just wondered if you were tired of playing it?

MARY: Not yet, Noel – I intend to beat him at it.

BYR: Now *that is* a dangerous game.

MARY: As you said, I'm in my element. *(she adjusts his stock).*

BYR: Touché, Mary! Just remember, should you lose to Shelley, you can always come and beat me…

MARY: I'll bear it in mind.

BYR: *That's* no place for a lover's proposition: reason extinguishes love.

MARY: That depends how hot it burns….

She smiles and exits. Enter the landlord, Byron hails him.

BYR: Padrone! I believe you have a room….

Fade

2.4

A small sailing-boat adrift on the sea. A week later. In the noonday sun Shelley, Trelawney and Clare lie on board, their arms hang over the side, fingers tracing the water.

SHEL: Cast adrift.

TRE: Becalmed.

CLA: We could be anywhere...

SHEL: We *are* anywhere.

TRE: Lost at sea.

CLA: Forgotten.

SHEL: Abandoned.

TRE: We could drift on forever.

CLA: Never returning home.

SHEL: Never needing one.

TRE: Pitching up anywhere.

SHEL: In our blue desert.

CLA: Nomads of the sea.

SHEL: Adventurers.

CLA: Buccaneers.

TRE: Fortune hunters!

SHEL: Who knows where we might end up?

CLA: India…

SHEL: The Orient…

TRE: Prison!

CLA: We'd escape.

SHEL: We *have* escaped.

CLA: And we're never going back.

TRE: We *are*… *(both turn to him)* The tide is taking us back in…

SHEL: It always does….

They drift on to the sound of distant song.

Fade.

2.5

A small annexe at the very top of Villa Mare. Later that evening. Mary sits meditatively. She hears footsteps and the sound of Shelley's voice calling: "Mary?" She doesn't respond, enter Shelley.

SHEL: I thought you might be up here…

Mary doesn't look up.

The room suits your mood.

MARY: Meaning what?

SHEL: Meaning, remote and inaccessible. - You don't have to stay here Mary – not in this room, not in Italy.

MARY: No?

SHEL: Not for a moment longer than you wish.

MARY: And where else can I go?

SHEL: Anywhere you like…Paris…London…

MARY: On my own? Very practical.

SHEL: Not on your own – I'd come with you.

MARY: Don't say things you don't mean, Percy.

SHEL: I do mean it. You know I wouldn't leave you to travel alone.

MARY: You'd…come back with me?

SHEL: Of course. Then, once you'd settled, I'd return.

MARY: I see. *(she moves to leave but Shelley bars her exit.)* Let me by Percy--

SHEL: Must I?

MARY: I'm not staying here to be made fun of--

SHEL: No, you'd rather make a fool of yourself elsewhere--

MARY: If it means getting away from you –!

SHEL: And why would you want to do that?

MARY: Because I won't be treated like a fool! You haven't the remotest concern for my opinion about anything that really matters!

SHEL: Mary--

MARY: It's true! If you did you'd leave this god-forsaken place--

SHEL: Paradise should be god-forsaken! Besides, Byron promises--

MARY: You're not listening! - The air, this place - why was it deserted? Why did the glorious Byrons abandon it? The clue's in the word, Shelley!

SHEL: What word? What are you talking about?

MARY: "Malaria!" The air's poisonous: people die here… Well you may not care about our children but I'm not taking any chances.

SHEL: No-one's going to die! Look, we've got Byron out here, with him on our side--

MARY: Oh yes, the man of the age! Where would we be without him! I'll tell you where: Rome, Paris, somewhere of our own choosing rather than his – that is, if you can bear to be without him for ten minutes. Sometimes I think you're half in love with him yourself!

SHEL: Shouldn't one love one's friends?

MARY: That's just it, Percy: you have your friends: you don't need me… and you can't love someone you don't need.

SHEL: You can *only* love someone you don't need. Love wouldn't make any sense otherwise.

39

MARY: Love doesn't have to make sense, Percy.

SHEL: Everything has to make sense! I do love you Mary– but don't ask me to leave… *(beat. Mary turns away.)* This room faces east; it'll catch the morning sun. You could make it your study.

MARY: It'd be too hot.

SHEL: Not in autumn.

MARY: True, because I won't be here then. *(silence)* One week.

SHEL: What?

MARY: To find somewhere new…

SHEL: Mary you're being--

MARY: Or I'll leave.

SHEL: All right - I'll start looking…

MARY: Swear.

SHEL: I promise…

MARY: On our children's lives.

SHEL: I swear that we'll leave – and that we'll be safe.
(he moves to take her in his arms but she turns away)

Slow fade.

2.6

*Byron's palatial new villa. A few days later. Morning.
Flushed with pleasure, he is experimenting with a new
épée whilst a groaning Fletcher goes back and forth
depositing trunks and cases.*

BYR: So, Fletcher! What d'yer think of my little bolt-hole? Ideal
for privacy but close to society when required - and weren't
the contessa's daughters delightful? I told you I had an ace
up my sleeve, did I not? A few simple enquiries amongst the
native aristocracy. Perfect! *(Fletcher doesn't reply)*
Fletcher? *(Fletcher plonks down another trunk nearby.)*

FLE: If you say so, milord.

BYR: You don't approve....

FLE: It's a nice enough place, milord--

BYR: But...? *(he flourishes the épée).*

FLE: Well, I just thought the whole point of being out here was to
be together - with the others, I mean.

BYR: Fletcher, do you never tire of being such a fool?
(he turns towards him & menaces him with the épée) -
indeed, perhaps you'd tell me once and for all where you did
learn to be so constantly - *(he swishes at Fletcher)* -
superlatively...stupid?

FLE: Milord..?

BYR: Well, what is the source of your folly, eh?

*Byron begins to poke Fletcher with the épée; Fletcher in
defence picks up a cushion.*

41

I only ask because I do so want to understand its roots -
whence it came to such full bloom *(grammatically
deliberate)* - in such an one as you?

FLE: Milord – please!

Byron raises the épée until it hovers under Fletcher's chin.

BYR: Then for god's sake try and understand, Fletcher - there is
breathing the fresh air of friendship - and there is being
suffocated by it! This is our home for the foreseeable future,
and what other kind of future is there...? *(Byron catches
sight of something in the distance and points his épée at it)*
Ah, I do believe we can just see Villa Mare there in the
distance! How disappointing. Still we shan't let that spoil the
view. Now, shall we have another look at the quality of the
locals! I do love a minor aristocrat for supper...

FLE: Tonight? We've no food, no servants and no-- !

BYR: Find'em Fletcher! Send out for them, but don't dawdle:
you've got duties to perform.

FLE: Miracles, more like.

BYR: Ah, loaves and fishes, Fletcher - loaves and fishes....

*Exit a grudging Fletcher. Byron resumes his languid
fencing practise.*

Fade.

2.7

Veranda of Villa Mare. Nightfall. A day or so later. A clear sky with a full moon. The air regulated by the more peaceful rhythm of Italian crickets. Clare gazes up at the stars, undistracted by Hayden's approach.

HAYD: So many stars…

CLA: Mm?

HAYD: And a moon so large you could almost steal it from the heavens…. Clare…?

CLA: Byron won't come back - I know it.

HAYD: *(exasperated)* Clare--!

CLA: Not now he's found somewhere new - and nothing will have changed…

HAYD: He'll be back. The emperor needs his empire and his servants: the question is, Clare, do they need him?

CLA: What are you talking about?

HAYD: Everything you've suffered, Clare - what you still suffer because of Byron.

CLA: I'm not suffering anything because of Byron! And since you seem to think it's your business you should know that everything I say or do with respect to Byron is a well-rehearsed act performed solely for Allegra's benefit!

HAYD: But there are ways of securing Allegra's future without him!

CLA: I'm sorry, but I really don't think you're qualified--

43

HAYD: Just listen a minute…I know I haven't said anything about this before, but I've done nothing but think about it all summer, I promise you. Every mountain, every meadow, every twist and turn of the road leads me to the thought of you, Clare, and I know I'm right: we could help each other--

CLA: Help each other?

HAYD: You need someone to care for you Clare - both you and Allegra. I know I haven't much money at the moment - but there's a strong chance I'll be elected to the Academy on my return--

CLA: Hayden, please--!

He grasps her arm.

HAYD: Promise you'll consider what I've said.

CLA: It won't make any difference. *(she breaks free)*

HAYD: Promise…

His gaze follows her as she exits.

Fade.

2.8

Byron's palazzo. Late morning. A few days later. The shuttered drawing-room. A village girl gabbles at Byron.

BYR: The female will, incarnate! *(mock courtly tones)* Don't talk to me like that, my dear – whatever it is you're saying! *(she continues)* Now look, unless you calm down I'm going to--

Enter Fletcher.

44

BYR: Yes, what is it?

FLE: Mr Shelley to see you milord.

Enter Shelley

BYR: Ah, the messenger of the gods – what news? We've missed you at our soirees - where've you been? No, don't answer that – sit down! *(snapping his fingers at Fletcher)* - Fletcher, some nectar for Mercury here! No, bring him a chair first. Now, how are you? No! First let me guess the purpose of your mission - don't tell me: you've come to save my soul.

SHEL: Or your virginity - *(looking at the girl who has fallen sullenly silent)* - whichever's in more danger.

BYR: My soul - unfortunately. My powers of persuasion in Italian seem to be sadly lacking. Leave us alone, my dear. Va via, per favore. *(the girl begins to remonstrate).* No arguments! We agreed the rules - if you can't keep them--!

As the girl leaves she sarcastically curtsies to Shelley.

GIRL: Buongiorno, milord, felice di conoscerla.

SHEL: Anch'io, signorina. *(Lightly bowing his head)*

GIRL: Ah finalmente un gentiluomo raffinato - lei me sembra--

BYR: Out, damn you!

Girl looks daggers at Byron & exits, nearly up-ending Fletcher's tray as he returns with cold drinks, after serving them, he exits.

SHEL: Interviewing new servants, Byron?

BYR: A heavy duty, Shel' – 'noblesse oblige' and all that: but speak to me! How goes Villa Mare, House of Shame? I trust the furniture I sent met with your approval?

SHEL: We were wondering when you'd return to enjoy it yourself?

BYR: Return? Hmm - you know, I don't think I shall be returning to Villa Mare. Truth is, Fletcher and I have rather settled into our little townhouse - not much of a townhouse, I admit, but then it's not much of a town! Still, since the contessa offered it to me for nothing it'd be churlish to refuse, would it not?

SHEL: And the rest of our arrangements?

BYR: Mm?

SHEL: The "Exiles' Review": - our 'voice in the wilderness...'

BYR: All in good time, Shelley, for god's sake, I'm not ready for scribbling yet.

SHEL: We've been here a fortnight.

BYR: A week, a month, a decade – what's the difference in a hot climate? Don't look so concerned: we'll get your anti-god, anti-government, anti-everything organ onto the streets before you can say--

Fletcher bursts in knocking on door as he does so.

FLE: It's a nun, Milord!

BYR: What?

FLE: Well - an 'oly woman of some sort!

BYR: Holy woman? What are you talking about?

46

FLE: 'ead to foot, Sir: white as a ghost: cape, shoes – and an 'ood!

BYR: Never mind her dress-sense, Fletcher – who the hell is she?

FLE: *(putting finger to lips and whispering)* Says she's an old friend of the family - an abbess! Adam-something--

BYR: Not – Dell'Adumbrina…?!

FLE: That's it! Abbess di Adum - thingy – of San something abbey!

BYR: Well show her up, Fletcher, show her up!

Exit Fletcher

Good God! Dell'Adumbrina! How you've risen in the ranks! She's English, Shelley - victim of the grand tour - took one look at the Sistine Chapel - converted on the spot! Bloody Michelangelo! Actually she was once rather attractive - for a nun. Tried to teach me the catechism as a child! And she plagued my aged uncle – used to lace his afternoon tea with fire and brimstone. In return he'd sweeten the sour old devil with donations to her damned abbey. Doubtless alms collecting is her holy mission here, too. Well, let's make her work for it, shall we? But I warn you, she's sharp!

Fletcher ushers in the Abbess.

Reverend Mother! My dear Mother Abbess Dell'Adumbrina! Excellent to see you again after so many years!

ABB: *(greeting them)* Signore, signore. *(she sits)* – Bentornato in Italia, Milord – welcome back! Indeed, it has been too many years since we saw the generous Byrons in our poor country. *(She arranges her robes decorously about her)*

BYR: Indeed too long, too long - Fletcher - a footstool!

ABB: You are much like your uncle, Milord. *(to Shelley)* – When last we met he was no more than a boy, Signore.

SHEL: So I hear, Madam.

ABB: A spoilt boy - with everything at his fingertips: but this, I will say, was many years ago.

SHEL: And yet how little time alters a man's essential character!

ABB: This too is true, signore. I see your friend knows you well, Milord: it is good to have such friends. But indeed I myself am not ignorant of your history. How could I be - when news of your success spreads throughout the courts of Europe?

BYR: The goddess fortune has indulged me, it's true Mother Abbess; but then, like all women, her favour brings its own troubles too.

ABB: Indeed, I hope for your sake, it is false what I have heard Milord, that so irresistible is the contagion of your fame that women have been known even to faint when you enter the room?

SHEL: Ah, Reverend Mother - the sick-list grows longer by the day.

ABB: Then we must hope the carrier of the virus remains immune himself, for it is too often a poet's weakness to court the public's love.

BYR: Ah, but the poet is an unwilling suitor, Abbess, the public seduces him and his reputation is nothing but, forgive the term, Reverend Mother, a bastard child born of their…

[Byron cont.]

(searching for words) - cheap adulation which he's then forced to father. Yes, there maybe some family likeness, but generally it goes its own wicked way, blackening the very name that gave it respectability - no, I'll admit no paternity of my reputation.

ABB: Then we can but hope you are not similarly indisposed towards you more...flesh and blood offspring, Milord!

BYR: I beg your pardon?

ABB: You have brought a daughter to Italy, have you not? Or must I apologise for giving an ear to the idle gossip of servants and peasants?

BYR: No, you need not as it happens - but what of it?

ABB: Merely that I thought Milord would wish to know of the facilities our new convent might offer for her education. We already provide schooling for several such young ladies, so she would not be alone. Lodging is, of course, compulsory, and comparatively cheap, and fees would be arranged at Milord's discretion, naturally.

BYR: Naturally.

ABB: But listen to me! Forgive me my Lord; we have barely encountered each other again after an interstice of many years. Of course, these are early days, but I merely thought it better to bring the matter to your attention now, so you could consider it amongst your many choices - one word and I can organise everything - it would be a shame, would it not, if little miss – er--?

SHEL: Allegra.

ABB: Allegra - si, a fine Italian name - if Miss Allegra were to miss out on her education while you sojourn here with us.

BYR: The question of her education has occupied my mind of late, I admit, though as to a convent, well…what do you think, Shelley? But then perhaps it's not fair to ask you under the circumstances, is it?

SHEL: Perhaps not.

ABB: Come now, milord – what circumstance can so invalidate a good friend's counsel?

BYR: Why - surely those same gossiping servants informed the Reverend Mother? No, I see not. Well, the fact is, my friend here…is an atheist.

The Abbess draws herself up bombastically.

Oh a very mild-mannered one, I promise you - respectable even.

ABB: Such a word can never be applied to infidels Milord! *(turns to Shelley)* And you, Signore – a few years ago you would have been made to repent for your sins.

BYR: Or been severely punished – eh Reverend Mother?

ABB: Indeed, Milord, he would have been burned at the stake!

The mood darkens.

SHEL: For my own good, no doubt.

ABB: No - for the safety of Our Lord's flock - the sheep must be protected from the wolf, Signore.

50

BYR: Exactly what I always tell him Reverend Mother - why, only the other day he tried to convince me, a god-fearing man, that Genesis was wrong: that neither the world nor time had any absolute beginning--

SHEL: That reason could prove or the senses perceive.

BYR: -And therefore needed no God to create them! He even tried to persuade me that the very word 'God' is just... a verbal disguise for fear - a superstition!

ABB: Is this blasphemy true, Signore?

Shelley sips his drink casually.

SHEL: I believe we make a god of what we don't understand, yes.

ABB: And that God in heaven did not create man after his own image?

SHEL: Actually, I'd say man made god after *his* own worst image - jealous, proud and vengeful.

ABB: Then perhaps you would tell us, Signore - and I argue only for the sake of redeeming you from profane error - perhaps you would tell us whom it is we have to thank for this world of plenty, this planet which supplies all our needs? You will at least admit it is a strange chance that man finds himself not only alive, but provided with everything he could desire: food and drink, not to mention the luxuries of beauty, of flowers and perfume--

SHEL: Nature supplies as many poisons as perfumes, Abbess - ask those who died in the discovery.

ABB: You know very well I speak of the design of the universe, signore! If such as you will not accept Almighty God in

51

[Abbess cont.]

person - *(she crosses herself)* - at least you cannot deny his attributes. *(Emphatic)* God's order is all around us in nature!

SHEL: What order would that be, Abbess? Earthquakes, floods, volcanoes? Not much design for poor old mankind there!

ABB: Punishments!

SHEL: Ah yes - where would religion be without punitive natural disasters to kill off a few babies and children! Sinners all!

BYR: *(nervously to Abbess)* The devil's advocate! - I can assure you my friend is a great lover of Mother Nature.

SHEL: Mother - more of an old hag, I'd say! What sort of woman murders her offspring, and sets one species to prey on another? Man hardly had a choice but to be vengeful; but then god must've foreseen that; after all he created Mother Nature - it would've been naive not to expect man to show some family likeness.

ABB: This is insupportable--

SHEL: So it is, Reverend Mother: why *would* god create such an ambiguous creature as good old Mother Nature? What is it that god wants from man, your grace? Sometimes I wonder if he knows himself.

ABB: The almighty is omniscient.

SHEL: Then perhaps he's just getting confused in his old age; after all: that omniscience must be hard work: maybe he's having second thoughts; maybe, in the conflict of his desires, god is beginning to experience what it's like - to be human...

52

Shelley moves to the French window, opens one of the shutters ajar, to gaze over the bay.

ABB: *(pointedly shading her face from the light)* Your friend, milord, is, like all poets: a mere peddler of riddles, a creature who never perpetrated one real action in his entire life!

SHEL: A poet's words are actions, Abbess; ideas change history, or hadn't you heard?

BYR: Shelley, I think perhaps it's time--

ABB: No Milord, let us hear your friend out, that his beliefs may damn him the more completely.

SHEL: *(moving back to the company)* My beliefs take the shape I imagine for them, Abbess: mankind orders chaos - without god there would still be man - without man there would be nothing!

ABB: But do you believe in nothing greater than yourself?

SHEL: I believe in *everything* greater than myself--

BYR: *(rises to close the shutters)* Human perfectibility - it's all the rage with London's intelligentsia, Mother Abbess.

ABB: A theory – in practice it means nothing.

SHEL: On the contrary, it means a new philosophy - without a god.

ABB: And you believe this in your heart of hearts?

SHEL: Where else should one's deepest convictions lie?

ABB: *(to Byron)* - Then I can but advise you Milord that you consort ill with such company! *(She prepares to leave)* - and

[Abbess cont.]

that those you love were best kept well away from one who thinks thus! Under no circumstances should you allow your daughter to keep this man's society, if I may presume to counsel you…

BYR: You won't stay for dinner, Reverend Mother?

ABB: I will not Milord; and I must ask that our next meeting take place in different company. Of course, I am most glad to make your acquaintance once again and hope we may discuss your daughter's education in less pernicious circumstances. Good evening to you, milord. *(she makes a desultory sign of the cross and exits. Shelley shrugs dismissively, and pours himself more wine. Byron, meanwhile, is now seething).*

SHEL: God bless the old witch!

BYR: And damn you, Shelley! You might at least've spared me the agony of her humiliation. The woman has influence; this is a Catholic country: they take their religion seriously!

SHEL: Do they have a choice?

BYR: Do they *need* a choice? What does it matter what men believe?

SHEL: What a man believes determines his happiness.

BYR: Then I believe in Fletcher - ignorance is bliss, Shelley! God how I hate religious disputation! So earnest and so futile! Call me spineless, if you like... *(musing)* I blame my mother: - beat the fear of the lord into my arse - when I think of how she used to..! *(calming himself)* - No, I refuse even to remember! Ha! You want to know where a man's mental

54

cowardice comes from? His inability to vandalise the church of childhood memory - to blaspheme at the altar of his mother!

SHEL: Then thank god all parents are not so catholic in their folly.

BYR: Amen.

SHEL: And that our children are free to despise our choice of gods!

BYR: Now there I feel the good Abbess would demur.

SHEL: Her and her damned convent! The idea of it for Allegra!

BYR: Oh surely it's not so bad.

Just then the door is barged open by Fletcher and the village girl who is struggling to gain access.

BYR: What in hell's name--!

GIRL: Lascia mi!...vecchio bastardo--!

Fletcher bars her way.

FLE: Stop that you little viper! I told you milord is busy!

She kicks his shins; he groans and is forced to let her go.

BYR: Never strike a women, Fletcher - how many times do I have to tell you?...Excuse me, won't you, Shelley: I must defend Fletcher's honour *(he goes to Fletcher's aid)*. Now, now signorina, I'm going to have to teach you a lesson. Help me hold the little baggage, Fletcher!

They all grapple.

SHEL: Byron…

BYR: Talk later, Shelley!

Shelley is left alone as Byron and Fletcher carry out the girl against a background of shrieks, groans and laughter. Shelley returns to the French window, casting the doors wide open, he steps out into the brilliant sunlight.

Slow fade.

2.9

Back at Villa Mare. Later that night. Holding a lantern, a dishevelled Shelley is sleepwalking to the balcony overlooking a moonlit sea. The low rhythm of the waves repeats. Also holding an assortment of candles and lanterns, Trelawney, Mary and Claire stand close by staring at Shelley who is increasingly agitated.

SHEL: There - in the waves…Allegra--!

CLA: Shelley - *(handing Mary her candle, she tries to grasp him)*

MARY: Leave him - it's worse if you wake him...

SHEL: Somebody help her! Allegra!

CLA: I can't bear it--!

SHEL: Why is nobody helping her!? *(starts to clamber over the balcony)*

CLA: Make him stop!

At this point Trelawney intercepts him and leads him back to a sofa. Shelley lies down and appears to fall asleep immediately. The others exchange glances.

TRE: Allegra…it's been on his mind - what Byron said--

CLA: No-one's taking her from me - do you hear? Not Byron, not Shelley - none of you!

Claire turns away from Trelawney. Enter Hayden.

HAYD: Is everything all right?

TRE: Shelley - sleepwalking.

HAYD: Please, Clare, let me keep you company.

CLA: There's no need—

HAYD: I insist.

Mary insinuates to Trelawney that they should retire.

TRE: Sleep'd be best thing for us all, I should've thought…

MARY: Goodnight, then. *(She and Trelawney exit)*

HAYD: Here, *(proffers another candle).* Strange the moon should be so bright, yet shed so little light.

CLA: Perhaps the task of illuminating our miserable world exhausts her; no-one could blame her for being repelled by us.

HAYD: Oh Clare - Byron's made you so world-weary… I wish I could - I *know* I could help you to--

CLA: Benjamin, *please… (she makes to go but he bars her way.)*

57

HAYD: If you'd only consent to be with me… *(she turns away)* - You know how fond I am of you…

CLA: Fond?

HAYD: More than fond… you know what I mean--

CLA: Byron told me he was 'fond' of me once. 'Fond' - used to mean 'foolish' once, didn't it? How ridiculous unrequited lovers are: prostrating themselves in front of idols who couldn't care less for their worship. Truth is, you can't make anyone love you…

Irritated, Hayden goes to the bookshelf and begins unloading books decisively, Claire stares at him curiously.

HAYD: Perhaps the others were right after all; perhaps it would be better to leave you alone for a while - completely alone.

Claire demurs.

Surely in the circumstances you wouldn't expect me to stay? This whole place is a farce! – Shelley's made it plain he intends to have everything his own way – his books, papers everywhere - not to mention the noise of his damned children - at least Byron's will afford me temporary privacy. Oh don't worry, I'll be looking for somewhere of my own… I had hoped you'd join me…well, I shan't waste any more of your time. I'll leave a message for Shelley; I'm sure my departure won't disturb him unduly.

At this point Mary re-enters.

MARY: I'm sorry – I couldn't sleep…

HAYD: Well, I'll say goodnight…

58

Taking up his box of books, he stops momentarily in the doorway, then is gone. Claire sighs in exasperation and glares accusatively at Mary.

CLA: Did you have to leave me with him?

MARY: I'm sorry. - Poor Benjamin - it's not his fault you're the woman of his dreams….

CLA: I've done all I can to discourage him--

MARY: *(ironically)* – What better way to capture his heart! *(beat)* - Anyway, you're too hard on him, he has prospects; he may be dull, but there's a lot to be said for dull men: you can rely on them -

CLA: To bore you to death--

MARY: To protect you.

CLA: Oh yes, stuck stifling with the Haydens of this world - I want a soul mate not a cellmate!

MARY: So you prefer the courtly treachery of a Byron!

Turning away, Claire is silently furious, then turns back.

CLA: Why should we have to choose? What if women weren't meant to have just one husband; what if we're meant to share their best qualities - like a male harem...just think: a community of men serving each and every one of our desires! Well why not? Why shouldn't we do whatever we want? That's why we came out here, wasn't it? To be completely free! To rid ourselves of all the rules! Imagine: it - it'd be heaven! *(beat)* Let's see! - Trelawney I'd have for his raw courage, you know: the sense that he'd fight off a lion for you!

MARY: And afterwards address you with profound courtesy, "I apologise for the beast's appalling growling, Ma'am"…

CLA : And then take you there and then!

MARY: And Byron….

CLA: Byron I'd have for all his worst qualities: his seductiveness, his touch, his flattery--

MARY: However brief…

They exchange glances

And Shelley?

CLA: Shelley? Ah but Percy's different!

MARY: *(Ironically)* You could say that.

CLA: Do you remember his first visit?

MARY: How could I forget!

CLA: In the middle of that great storm!

MARY: Hammering on the door!

CLA: Like a madman!

MARY: Framed in the doorway, lightning all round!

CLA: Father thought he was a lunatic.

MARY: Mother did too - almost turned him away!

CLA: Long hair blown all over his face!

MARY: Like a character from a gothic novel!

CLA: Escaped from Bedlam!

MARY: 'Beware his flashing eyes! His floating hair!'

CLA: 'For he on honeydew hath fed and drunk the milk of paradise!'

MARY: And in he came – wet through!

CLA: Bringing the storm with him.

MARY: Like having an electrical charge in the room!

CLA: What an evening! Father waffling on about politics - and Shelley and you making eyes at each other behind his back.

MARY: We were not!

CLA: I was so jealous!

MARY: You didn't show it.

CLA: Of course not! Big sister! Last thing I was going to admit.

MARY: Well, no doubt we were all young and foolish--

CLA: Whereas now we're all old and wiser...

MARY: Or not.

CLA: Well one thing's for sure: life would be quite unliveable without Percy!

MARY: You should've married him.

CLA: You got there first... *(recovering herself)* So - who does that leave us with?

MARY: Fletcher!

CLA: Dear old Fletcher - I'd keep him for his comical irritability!

MARY: And Hayden?

CLA: Oh all right: Hayden we'd keep for those desperate moments when the others were all too tired! Ah, dreams: what would we have without them?

MARY: Reality. *(pause)* Have you ever thought that our companionship will be the only constant thing in our lives...? I *do* fear the future, Claire. What will we do when we're old, and they're...well, women always outlive their men!

CLA: We'll live together in an aged, virginal sisterhood!

MARY: Fine prospect--

CLA: Spending our days in eulogies of loves gone by! But not yet! There's plenty of time to be old in! *(she moves to window.)* Look! Trelawney! Let's go for a midnight swim! Come on!

She disrobes down to her petticoat and pulls Mary by the hands towards the door, Mary resists.

Spoilsport!

Claire exits, leaving Mary gazing by the window. The sound of laughter, Mary waves, then turns away disconsolately. Fade.

2.10

Villa Mare kitchen. Next morning. The sound of a child crying in another room and then being comforted. Mary enters to find Elise flirting with an Italian servant who quickly disappears about his business.

MARY: Couldn't you hear Allegra crying?

ELISE: *(pointedly)* I thought her mother was with her...

MARY: Mistress Clare has a chill, as you know. May I also ask when we can expect a meal today?

ELISE: There's nothing to cook, no oil, no meat, nothing, madame--

MARY: We don't eat meat, as you also know, Elise. Fish will do.

ELISE: Oh yes, I'll go and catch one, madame - and cook and clean and look after the children: - it's too much for one woman, as madame would find out if she tried.

MARY: If you don't like it here, you can always seek another post elsewhere, Elise, you have only to notify us. I suggest you think about it. I shall be in the drawing-room.

On this note of discord Mary exits, crossing with the Italian manservant carrying a log-basket. Elise throws off her pinafore.

ELISE: I'll not wait on her another minute - I'll not wait on anyone!

SERV: Beh! The angry Elise will run away, eh? Find an 'andsome prince? Magari! They're all ugly around here – and poor. Si! Brutissimi e poverissimi! Mi racommando!

He approaches her and strokes her hair. She shrugs him off.

ELISE: Not all of them…

She straightens her hair sensually, coquettishly. Manservant goes to kiss her, she turns her face away.

Slow fade.

2.11

Byron and Polidori on a sunlit strip of beach. Late that afternoon. Byron's arm is raised, he holds a cocked pistol – they have set up a shooting range. Fletcher reloads their pistols. They shoot alternately and so punctuate each other's remarks.

BYR: Boredom..! *(shoots)* - That's the thing.

He languidly hands pistol to Fletcher.

POLI: What thing?

BYR: The thing…

Interrupted by Polidori's shot

The thing that drives us to the tedious excess called 'sin.'

POLI: And what would a dilettante like you know about real sin, Byron?

BYR: Very little, actually, but I'm always willing to learn – and what better tutor is there than - *(shoots)* - boredom! Put these pop-guns away will you Fletcher, they're unusable - and fetch provender while you're about it. No, Polly! Boredom is

64

[Byron cont.]

the first cause of everything, the Primum Mobile of fate! It's why we go to bed, get up, make plans, money, conversation, love, enemies - everything! Show me the man who can sit alone in his room day after day doing absolutely nothing. Why, the very act of thought is just a flight from the stark prison of an empty mind.

Fletcher hands out food and wine.

Boredom, I tell you! We should be grateful to it! Without it what else would've stirred this dismal clay? Look what children do when they're bored: play with mud! The good lord himself probably stuck us together during a dull moment in paradise – a dubious achievement.

POLI: Such disenchantment, Byron – when you have everything you could possibly need: wine, new companions - I refer, of course, to your new, best friend - how is the lovelorn Hayden this morning?

BYR: Whining mongrel - crazy to offer him a kennel!

POLI: Er, Byron-- !

He coughs to alert Byron to the approach of Clare, who is collecting shells in an improvised 'basket' of her dress, however, Byron remains unaware.

BYR: Should've left him to pine for his bitch of a--!

POLI: Good afternoon Miss Claremont - this is a pleasant surprise.

CLA: Oh, I'm sorry--

POLI: Oh, don't apologise, please! We welcome the diversion. We were just talking about you as it happens…

Byron looks exasperated.

CLA: Really? Nothing pleasant, I hope.

POLI: Ah, now you're being ironic, which is a very unfair trick for a young lady to play on a gentleman - specially one as overheated as me--

BYR: Your perfervid temperature is of no interest to a lady, Polly… *(a momentary awkward silence ensues.)*

POLI: Well, more vino… *(he goes to fetch wine)*

CLA: Pretty shells on this part of the shore.

BYR: Very pretty; one might make a necklace of them - if one were in love--

CLA: And of course, you're not.

BYR: No, not just now, thank you, thank god.

CLA: I didn't know the almighty was interested in your romances.

BYR: Ah, well: god wouldn't be human if he didn't enjoy a bit of gossip now and then.

She doesn't smile.

CLA: Don't you think your irreligious posturing is a bit hypocritical?

BYR: What would you have one do - dance around town waving atheistical pamphlets like Shelley --?

66

CLA:	I wouldn't have you 'do' anything... In fact the less you do, the happier everyone else seems to be.
BYR:	You included, no doubt.
CLA:	I depend on you for nothing!
BYR:	That must be why you hounded me across half a continent.
CLA:	You were different then. You were worth pursuing.
BYR:	Well, you caught me, Claire - not my fault if I wasn't quite the catch you expected: you should've taken a closer look before you began the chase. But then, of course, love is blind.
CLA:	I never loved you.
BYR:	The lack of feeling's mutual, I assure you.
CLA:	I loved the stranger who wrote your poetry; who spoke - and wrote - from the heart; who was honest with himself, with his feelings.
BYR:	Ah yes, of course: feelings! Where would you women be without that prize possession! God knows, all the pride of your sex goes into your bloody sentiments! Parading them around in public like personal adornments: to be admired but never touched. Well let me tell you: feelings aren't just for display - and they don't survive unless they can take manhandling; weak hearts are made to be broken; that's what they're there for, Clare. They get replaced by stronger vessels. If I broke yours, I've done you a service. You'll see that one day.
CLA:	Spoken like a true cynic!

BYR: The truth *is* cynical.

CLA: It is in your mouth…you make everything sound worthless. Why do you bother: if you really feel life is so futile why do you even get out of bed in the morning?

BYR: I don't, since you ask: I make it a point of principle never to rise before one in the afternoon. Daylight is for dullards and their duties: I diminish it - and them - by staying up late. Night is far more mysterious.

CLA: So that's it: just laugh at everything, scorn everything, everyone.

BYR: I can think of less honest philosophies that fools have lived and died for.

CLA: So what *would* you live and die for exactly?

BYR: Good question: let me think. Fame? Over-rated. Wealth? Yes, money's fun, I can't deny it - but die for it? Hmm… Pleasures of the flesh..? Ten a penny. Love? Now there's a thing. Love. Yes there was a time when I was mad enough to think I'd die for that mutable mirage of an emotion…

CLA: So now love doesn't even exist?

BYR: Not in the way you'd like to think.

CLA: And what way is that?

BYR: The way that flatters a woman's pride.

CLA: You mean the way that compels you to feel anything. You know what I think?

BYR: No, do tell me.

68

CLA: I think you've become so terrified of what love might mean you daren't feel anything anymore.

BYR: I feel what I feel, when I feel it, Clare: nothing more nor less! I won't pretend sentiments I don't possess.

CLA: And the man who wrote your lyrics, the one full of ideals?

BYR: He's learned to keep himself to himself. As I suggest you do.

CLA: I'll never be like you.

BYR: No, no - that you never shall....

CLA: I'd rather die!

BYR: Typical woman: divert the argument and make your personal fate the subject of a philosophical debate when it suits you.

CLA: Forgive me, I thought philosophy *was* about people? You're just a coward.

BYR: A coward whose house you're living in.

CLA: Not for much longer. I don't want anything to do with it - or you.

BYR: How refreshing - and presumably this new 'attitude' extends to Allegra's education...!

CLA: Allegra's education, as you have made perfectly plain, is my business--

BYR: Ah yes, I see it now - the poor girl paying out her girlhood on the beach, consorting, naked, with the local savages--!

CLA: What concern is it of yours who she consorts with!

BYR: Young English ladies, wherever one finds them, should be groomed for the cultivated society of their origins - not that of...local women: Allegra won't thank you for your 'liberality.'

CLA: And yet no doubt *your* 'liberality' has been the toast of the very same local women you profess to scorn.

BYR: Clare, Clare - when will you learn that verbal tennis doesn't constitute a conversation - personally I never liked the sport in the first place - now if you'll excuse me - and for future reference, please consider this section of the beach your sole preserve. *(bows curtly and calls to Polidori and Fletcher)* Gentlemen!

He exits. Polidori and Fletcher sheepishly pass in front of Clare, who is left on the shore. Slowly and dejectedly, she lets fall the shells she has gathered.

Fade.

2.12

Shelley and Mary's bedroom. That night. A dry electrical storm. Lightning flares in the room. Shelley talks mechanically in his sleep. Mary wakes. He screams.

SHEL: Give me your hand!

MARY: Percy - wake up!

SHEL: Help me!

He looks terrified and grabs her arm.

MARY: Percy - you're hurting me! For god's sake!

She wrenches her arm free, he wakes and looks at her.

SHEL: I'm sorry…

MARY: Why do your dreams have to be so violent? It's horrible…

SHEL: I can't help my dreams.

MARY: I can't bear this anymore.

> *She sits on the bedside. He gets up and wanders to the window. Sees an old glass of wine, swigs it down. Breathes deeply.*

SHEL: I'll sleep in another room - it'll do us both good - to sleep alone *(beat),* eat alone, too, perhaps - occasionally, I mean.

MARY: Why not permanently? That's what you want.

SHEL: I'm just saying solitude is natural: we're born alone, we die--

MARY: Yes, yes – I've heard the solitude sermon.

SHEL: So we might as well get used to it.

MARY: But we don't have to *live* in it.

SHEL: If we want things to *be* different, we have to *live* differently, Mary! Just talking about it won't create a new world.

MARY: And what if I prefer the old one!

> *(Pause)*

SHEL: It doesn't work.

MARY: Does this?

SHEL: One day there'll be a new kind of love.

MARY: Oh of course--

SHEL: And a more humane version of man.

MARY: Created by you.

SHEL: All of us - poets, painters, philosophers.

MARY: All playing at being god--

SHEL: Not playing - doing what art does on a grand scale: Shakespeare created Hamlet!

MARY: He *wrote* Hamlet, Percy--

SHEL: And is he any less real in our imagination? It can be done. Isn't that what all philosophies worth their salt say anyway? You have to lose your self, step into the void, re-create yourself?

Lightning.

So beautiful. The time for childish terrors is over. *(watching the storm)* - what would it be like if we could stand in the lightning?

(pause)

MARY: Your plan wouldn't work. Man would re-create himself with all the faults of the original, and none of the virtues. You over-estimate the species, Percy: man needs limitations - he's a small creature.

SHEL: He can grow.

MARY: Not *that* much: infinity is terrifying.

SHEL: Well…we'll never know 'til we try.

MARY: And when we've tried and failed?

SHEL: Come back to bed: I promise to stop impersonating lunatics.

MARY: I can't sleep. I think I'll write a while…Just an idea - an idea about a man who tries to create another human being….

Exit Shelley, leaving Mary gazing out at the lightning and distant thunder.

2.13

Next day. Byron's bedroom. Mid-morning. Byron is sitting up in bed. Elise is seated by him, carelessly clothed in one of his gowns.

ELISE: I must go

BYR: You shall not!

ELISE: I left the child playing alone--

BYR: Good for her imagination!

ELISE: And if I should lose my position..?

BYR: Why then, my Swiss princess, you should gain one infinitely more pleasant with me here or elsewhere. Padua's nice, this time of year – Venice, without the tourists - or the water! Or perhaps Milan! Turin! Well? Fancy a miniature grand tour?

At this point Fletcher enters backwards as if prohibiting someone's entrance.

73

[Byron cont.]

What in hell's name - get out Fletcher, I didn't ring!

Enter Shelley carrying a riding crop, brushing Fletcher and his protests aside.

FLE: Mister Shelley, sir: enquiring after Mistress Elise and her charge, I shouldn't wonder. I told him you was engaged.

BYR: There! Fletcher's made a respectable couple of us – albeit with execrable grammar! Do come in, Shel', join the happy throng.

SHEL: You must make a better liar of your manservant, Byron.

BYR: Yes, his inadequacies are manifold, maybe I should just sack him.

SHEL: Maybe I should just sack my children's nurse – and who is looking after the child, Elise?

BYR: Come now Shel' - who's it hurting, after all? Her charge is playing happily in the garden; and I've frequently told you how charming I found the lady.

SHEL: Yes, you've always been most frank, Byron. Can we talk in private?

BYR: How much more private can you get, Shelley?

Elise rises but Byron restrains her.

You have just invaded my bedroom!

SHEL: Surely the least private of all your rooms!

BYR: On the contrary, it's been the scene of many intimate meditations on the redemptive power of love.

SHEL: Love! And which particular definition had you in mind this time, Byron? Do tell us--

BYR: Another time - I'm not in the mood for a discourse.

SHEL: No? What happened to your intimate meditations? Sit down Fletcher, Elise – let's listen to the expert.

BYR: *(coldly, with a hint of anger)* Deference itself, unfortunately for once you find me speechless.

SHEL: Then let me put words in your mouth Byron – let's see, love, love--

BYR: A bit repetitive aren't we?

FLE: He's thinking, Milord.

Byron is exasperated, Shelley turns suddenly.

SHEL: Love is above all a fraud! A master of self-deceit. He seduces himself to any cause - the more flippant and fleeting the better! - Tell me Byron, are you going to marry our humble Elise? She has a hell of a temper!

Byron bridles.

Or did you mean a more fraternal form of love; friendship, loyalty and all that! How *is* Hayden by the way? Or have you already thrown him out?

BYR: *(sarcastically)* I think our 'philosopher' begins to miss the mark.

SHEL: No, of course, you must've meant paternal love - incidentally, your daughter shows as little inclination for solitary prayer and reflection as you do Byron - perhaps you'd bear that in mind when you consider a convent education for her.

BYR: I'll thank you to exclude my daughter from your fatuous verbosity--

SHEL: As you exclude her from your life - but then doubtless your 'love,' like your god, moves in mysterious ways.

BYR: My religion and my 'love' are my affair--

SHEL: And your affairs are my business, no Elise? *(as she remains silent he turns to Fletcher)*. Fletcher? What do you think? Should we not be our brother's keeper?

FLE: Well... depends if he's keeping anything for *us*--

SHEL: Or *from* us--

BYR: D'you accuse me of deceit?!

SHEL: Why, are you guilty of it?

BYR: I'm guilty of nothing, damn you!

SHEL: Then nothing is what I accuse you of - that and your ignorance on the subject of love--

BYR: Fuck love!

A charged silence which Shelley breaks by making to leave.

SHEL: I'll see myself out, Fletcher. *(to Elise)* I feel sure Allegra's mother will be expecting her daughter back, Elise – when you can spare a moment, of course. But then perhaps I should take her back myself--!

BYR: You can leave that responsibility to me, Shelley – as you suggest: I am still her father, after all!

Shelley glares at Byron and exits, contemptuously leaving the door wide open.

BYR: Don't say it, Fletcher!

FLE: What, milord?

BYR: Anything! Good god, I will not be lectured to! Shelley and his ideal world! A quid-pro-quo arrangement just like any other, that's what love is - a mask for bare-faced selfishness!

At this point Hayden diffidently enters the room.

What do *you* want?

HAYD: What on earth's wrong with Shelley - just cut me dead!

FLE: Milord and mister--

BYR: *(instantaneously adapts his mood)* A minor disagreement about my daughter's education, if you must know. All sorted out now. *(Fletcher looks confused)* – Allegra's staying here to begin tutelage, I've hired someone: Shelley's not keen but I've insisted. Just tying up a few loose ends. After all, the child's mother has always insisted I should pay for a decent education

HAYD: Suppose it makes as much sense as anything around here.

Byron smiles as Hayden exits, then quickly turns to Fletcher.

BYR: Prepare the horses, Fletcher!

ELISE: Where are we going?

BYR: *We're* not going anywhere, my dear - at least, *you* aren't: Fletcher and I are going to see the Abbess. Allegra needs an education - I'm providing one - but not here… Oh I know it's a cliché but everything happens for a reason - the Abbess is famous for her prophetic powers: she must've seen my money coming a mile off!

ELISE: And Mr Hayden?

BYR: Oh I don't think we need to need to complicate matters - the fellow's confused enough as it is!

ELISE: You'll be back soon?

BYR: Of course - and then I'll sweep you off to Venice or Rome or - wherever you want!... Promise!

Exit Byron, followed by Fletcher who casts a baleful glance at Elise before closing the door.

Fade.

End of Act Two.

ACT 3. Sc 1

The main gate to the local convent. Early afternoon that same day. Byron paces about. Fletcher enters.

FLE: It weren't wise, milord – bringing her here so sudden in this heat.

BYR: If this haste appears unseemly, Fletcher, you'd do well to remember it was forced upon me by accusations of indolence and delay!

FLE: But she's running a real temperature--

BYR: Then the sooner we get her settled here the better! You think I'm cruel, don't you Fletcher? But I refuse to be imprisoned by anyone else's beliefs - especially Shelley's! A theory for this, an ideal for that: skewering everything with his logic - like a bloody lepidopterist - well there's a reason life won't be pinned down: it decays! Everything rots - love quicker than anything! God knows, his own marriage ought to have taught him that! *(beat)* Where are these holy fools - they can't all be tending sacred gardens, for god's sake!?

A nun, Sister Paola answers through the gate's grating.

Ah, finally! Buonasera! Mi chiamo Lord Byron, sono venuto a presentare…. Look! I've come to deliver my daughter to the Reverend Mother! She's to be educated at the convent.

NUN: I am sorry, milord - we have had no notice--

BYR: Please don't waste my time! Byron! The name is Byron! It was the Abbess dell'Adumbrina's personal recommendation.

Sis. P: Ah, si..! Milord Byron! Ma senz'altro! I fetch the Reverend Mother. Un momentino, per favore….

She goes off. Byron paces irritably.

BYR: For god's sake stop moping around, Fletcher!

FLE: She needs a doctor--

BYR: The devil she does – the child's just over-heated that's all!

At this point the Abbess appears accompanied by Sis. P.

Ah Abbess, good evening to you! I've brought my daughter.

ABB: Ah, yes, but I recognised your coach a long way off, milord - my eyesight is as sharp as the eagles around here. I am pleased to see you, of course, and curious too: you gave us little warning--

BYR: A change of circumstances - a change of plan regarding my daughter's education. I trust the lack of advertisement presents no problem.

ABB: But how should it. Milord? The house of the lord is always open, especially to children, no? She's in the coach?

FLE: She's not well.

Byron is exasperated.

ABB: Not well – no fever, I hope? It has already carried off one child, and a young novice also, I believe?

Sister Paola nods.

BYR: I assure you Abbess, she is hot and bothered, nothing more.

ABB: Then we had best remove her to a place of shade, had we not, sister? Indeed, shade is something we have in abundance

80

here. The cloistered life! No, she will not want for shade, that much I can say.

BYR: Then if everything's in order I shall waste no more of your time, Abbess. I wish only to confirm that the girl is to have as 'catholic' an education as your resources may afford.

ABB: But of course - and how glad I am, milord, that our mother country's protestant falsehoods find no allegiance in your own heart.

BYR: Forgive me, mother Abbess, but I worship the deity not his dress. All outward forms of religion are alike to me. The fact is my daughter finds herself in Rome and must do as the Romans. Were she in India I should doubtless choose the Hindu for her model!

ABB: Ah the British sense of humour, how I miss my own people sometimes, milord!

BYR: You'll send your bills to my bankers of course; and I want to know how the girl settles down. Byrons are not good at fitting in: if she can't adapt I'll think of something else. Meanwhile she's to receive no visitors - apart from her mother, she can come when she wants; but certainly not Mister Shelley...

ABB: Do I infer that milord has fallen out with this infidel?

BYR: Infer what you like, Mother Abbess, but keep him away from my daughter.

ABB: With pleasure, milord - god be with you.

BYR: Thank you - but I fear I'll have to make do with Fletcher! Come on, Fletcher, this place is stifling. I fancy a swim!

ABB: Ah but milord, how wonderful to be able to act on such whims! I almost feel I could come with you - oh don't look so alarmed - just a joke *(crosses herself)* the good Lord forgive me - you see what a wicked influence you have, milord! An old lady of the cloth in the sea with Lord Byron!

BYR: Well, quite. Not sure my own reputation would survive, Mother Abbess! You'll let me know how my daughter goes on?

ABB: But of course, don't worry another moment, milord. Enjoy your swim!

Exit Byron and Fletcher – the Abbess turns to the nun.

(coldly) Bring the girl forward to me....

Fade.

3.2

Villa Mare's drawing-room. Later that day. An irate Shelley paces about in front of a seated Clare. Trelawney stands behind her chair. Two other servants stand apprehensively nearby. The atmosphere is tense.

SHEL: *(incredulously)* She'll just make things worse!

TRE: *(Coolly)* She wouldn't listen; she went straight to Byron as soon as Fletcher sent word – I thought I should stay with Claire.

CLA: I don't need looking after - I just want Allegra back! For god's sake why didn't you bring her back with you Shelley!?

SHEL: *(pacing, head in hands)* There was no mention of the convent; Elise was there, Allegra was playing in the garden—I thought--

TRE: Mary swears she won't come back without her.

SHEL: I'm going to the Convent!

TRE: I'll come with you! *(to Claire)* So long as you'll be alright…

CLA: Go! *(Shelley and Trelawney leave)* – Just bring her back!

Exit Shelley and Trelawney. Claire turns and goes to the balcony and looks out.

Fade.

3.3

The beach. Same time. Mary enters stage left to find Byron sunning himself on a rock, naked. Seeing her, he puts a towel around himself, rises and offers her a hand, which she disdains.

BYR: Mary… what kept you? Don't be silly, take my hand! I saw you coming - thought I'd better wait: didn't want you to think I was trying to escape: you're the last woman I'd run from!

MARY: Spare me your idiotic flattery.

BYR: Oh Mary, don't be angry, it's too hot for that.

MARY: *(half averting her gaze)* I've come for Allegra.

BYR: Really, I had hoped it was for more personal reasons…

He starts to dress

MARY: Why, Byron; why would you do such a thing? To cause pain, is that it? Prove your power?

BYR: I assume we're talking about my daughter's education. I am her father after all...or so they tell me.

MARY: Don't be absurd: you know she's yours!

BYR: Her and a half a dozen others this side of the Alps! Look, I'm sorry, Mary: I sent my daughter to a convent because I thought it best! At least you may console yourself in the knowledge that Allegra will receive a real education, not one formed from half-baked ideas. That's your trouble: you Shelleys live in the abstract - I deal with the cut and thrust of the real world. Life is war, Mary; holy or unholy, the battle of the sexes is no metaphor, what women lack in strength they make up for in cunning. Not that I blame them: contrary to what you may think, I *don't* wish to be cruel, and I have no particular desire – or need – to be powerful, as you suggest; god knows, I leave all that rubbish to my idiotic so-called 'peers' in the House of Lords. All I've done is accept my responsibilities! The fact is: your sister pursued me - I'm not complaining: I don't mind being pursued - as long as I'm allowed to surrender - or escape - when it suits me. *(beat)* The game of romance only extends so far. If your sister can't tell when it's over that's her lookout. Her trouble is she reads too much poetry.

MARY: *(coldly)* And you write too much of it.

BYR: *(equally so)* No doubt.

MARY: Everything you say is for effect – I don't think you know what a sincere moral act is.

BYR: Never said I did, Mary: morality is a mystery to me, at least your version of it. But then surely that's the point: one man's meat, et cetera. To me it's all a matter – of perspective: *(he gazes seaward)* as I say: the abstract versus the actual – just as in dear old mother nature herself.

MARY: What's nature got to do with it?

BYR: A view of the sea is different from actually swimming in it: the reality's colder; some of the creatures in it are unfriendly.... One's view of experience depends on where one stands, Mary. You can't deny you had a view of this place before we came out here. You expected things to go a certain way; well it's hardly my fault if circumstance took a diversion.

MARY: It's entirely your fault--

BYR: What is? Pursuing my own interests? If I pursued yours, that would make me moral, would it? For god's sake you Shelleys are so blinded by sanctimony you can't see straight!

MARY: I can see a little girl feeling desolate, with no-one but those vindictive old virgins for company. How could you?! You know what those places are like!

BYR: Oh Harrow wasn't so bad: there weren't any nuns, for a start! Look, Mary, I don't wish to appear flippant but you bring it out in me; you're so very...earnest.... Did you but know it I have no quarrel with you: go and get her if you want. I'll write a letter or something.

MARY: She's *your* daughter!

BYR: And I shall do right by her.

MARY: You could start by admitting you love her....

Byron avoids her gaze.

I've seen you together: I've seen a father's look in those eyes.

BYR: *(sardonically)* A look of shock, you mean!

MARY: - of protection, real responsibility for a vulnerable child who depends on you.

BYR: And you can tell all that from a glance?

MARY: You can't deny it.

BYR: I can deny anything if I try hard enough, I assure you. *(beat)* But I won't deny she's a winning creature. I like her well enough.

MARY: And she unites our families…

BYR: So that's the plan!

MARY: I mean she brings us all closer together--

BYR: - which is precisely what I've always been worried about.

MARY: Not you and Claire: my sister accepts the …liaison between you is over: she's glad it is! *(Byron snorts)* I mean you and Shelley - and me. We'd have a reason to remain friends - more than friends…

BYR: Do we need a reason?

She approaches him

MARY: No… we don't…

86

Suddenly she kisses him. He responds. The kiss ends. Mary disengages, turns away, trying to hide her confusion.

BYR: You and I, we might have been - still could be--

MARY: *(muted)* Don't say anything.

Byron draws her back to him and they kiss again. They lie down together, he takes her in his arms, they kiss again. There is a natural pause in their lovemaking.

MARY: This is wrong…

BYR: And the sweeter for it. *(he kisses her again)*

MARY: Please…

BYR: Isn't love free? Why feel guilty for living out Shelley's philosophy? Surely he'd applaud us. Anyway, guilty pleasures are the best kind.

MARY: And that's all it is to you.

BYR: Now did I say that?

MARY: No but you meant it.

BYR: So one kiss and suddenly you know what's in my mind as well as my heart…

MARY: No. - I don't understand you at all.

Byron sits up and stares.

BYR: I don't understand myself, Mary; but then I don't feel the need to - not anymore; to hell with Greek oracles!

[Byron cont.]

Knowing thyself is a fruitless task. How *can* one know oneself when one changes so frequently? You might be one person one day, feel one way, and then quite the opposite the next. And why not? What could be more boring than being the same person day after day?

MARY: And constancy? Fidelity to the people one loves?

BYR: - Lasts as long as one loves them - anything else is sheer pretence - or 'marriage' to give it its formal name.

MARY: So love never lasts in your book?

BYR: I don't say it can't; just that it doesn't - most of the time. Lovers must keep each other interested: love needs fuel added to the fire or it goes out. It has something to do with independent lives…

MARY: …What am I to say to Claire?

BYR: Don't say anything.

MARY: Deceive her, you mean.

BYR: Is silence a lie?

MARY: If it withholds the truth.

BYR: Then tell her the truth.

MARY: Which is what?

BYR: That you and I… are deeply attracted to each other, just as she and I once were.

88

MARY: As simple as that.

BYR: As simple as Claire is prepared to let it be.

MARY: You don't know Claire: we're sisters, for god's sake!

BYR: Then there's nothing you can't tell each other...

MARY: Except this *(she makes to leave)*...

BYR: You'll come and see me again soon?

MARY: Unless I can stop myself.

BYR: Ha! Sphinx-like to the end!

MARY: You'll bring Allegra back?

BYR: Yes, yes - go and get her yourself! I told you I'll write
          something now - whatever you want...

MARY: Thank you. I must get back, tell Claire the good news!

BYR: About us?

MARY: About her...*your*...daughter.

BYR: Promise me you'll come back soon - before I change my
          mind – a lover's prerogative, no?

          He kisses her hand. She retracts it, then leaves slowly.

          Fade.

3.4

The Abbey. Same day – late afternoon. The Abbess walks across the stage. Sister Paola, accompanies her.

ABB: Is it definitely the fever...?

Sis. P: The child has the same rash, Reverend Abbess.

ABB: Then she is a danger to us all - as if we had not sufficient troubles...this is the devil's work. I should never have insulted the blessed virgin by accepting a child from an infidel mother.... Now she punishes us by bringing up contagion from the valleys. The girl cannot stay! Take her to la signora Rosetta.

Sis. P: Reverend mother?

ABB: Her ways are best in these matters. Besides we can do nothing here but pray for her soul... See to it also that milord Byron is informed of this, sister - and lose no time - the sooner the child is outside our gates the sooner our sin is expiated...

The Abbess kneels and crosses herself.

If she recovers then it is also a sign and we can accept her back again. Go – hurry!

She closes her eyes in prayer. Exit nun.

Fade.

3.5

An osteria. Early that evening. Simple wooden tables and benches. Byron, sundry ex-pats and local Italians are all in their cups. Byron plays to the gallery throughout the following. Fletcher is idly holding Byron's fencing épées.

BYR: Gentlemen, a toast: to the weaker sex! – I mean men, of course.

POLI: Well, Elise has certainly wrapped you round her little finger, Byron.

BYR: Poor girl – never heard of a metaphor: - convinced I'll take her back to England and make a real queen of her! And so I shall - when I'm king myself!

POLI: Royally spoken Byron! A toast to the king of parvenus!

BYR: What? Do you doubt the colour of my blood? We Byron's go back to the Normans--!

VOICE: Why?

POLI: To get them to keep quiet about the bastards in the family! By the way, Byron: how's your daughter?

BYR: I tire of your feeble wit, Polly.

POLI: No more than we of your feebler boasts.

BYR: Right ! – Fencing practise Fletcher!

Fletcher passes épées. Byron throws an épée to Polidori and thrusts at him mockingly in same moment –

Have at you Pollydolly!

A drunk Polidori is pushed, prodded and prinked around the table throughout the following.

A lesson in nobility for you, good doctor! There's more blue blood in my little finger than surgeon's art in the whole of that bloated, tumescent corpse you call a body!

Byron finally winds him, bending him double and then sticks him in the bottom, sending him tumbling. Amidst the cheers, Byron salutes in correct épée style. He is about to sit down when Hayden enters.

BYR: Ah Hayden, do please come and join us – or better still – fuck off.

HAYD: You lied to me, Byron.

BYR: I beg your pardon? *(he casually pours himself more wine)*

HAYD: About your daughter - you stole her--!

BYR: Kidnapped my own daughter? Now that's a first for any father!

HAYD: You lied!

BYR: No… I gave you half the truth, Hayden.

HAYD: Why?!

BYR: Why? A half-truth for a half-hearted fellow – and to what do we owe this derring-do – nothing to do with the damsel Claire, I suppose?

HAYD: Damn you, Byron!

As he approaches, Byron raises his épée.

BYR: No? Don't tell me you've suddenly developed a backbone, Hayden! Look, he's even learned to stand up straight: perhaps there is something in Shelley's notion of human perfectibility after all!

HAYD: You can mock all you want--

BYR: Yes, I can, can't I. But then you're such an easy target one can hardly claim the praise, Hayden. Indeed, gentlemen, consider the species, 'Hadyensius patheticus', so very mockable ain't he? *(Byron's épée prods around Hayden)* What with his naivety in love and his neuralgia out of it, he made a rare and woeful beast...

A half-drunk Polidori raises his head blearily.

POLI: Made...?

BYR: I use the past tense because he represents the last of his kind: extinction is inevitable, gentlemen! No known female of the species survives--

POLI: Shame.

BYR: Not really - they made an awful whining noise - particularly in courtship. Is't not so, Hayden? Tell us now, what is it that draws two such sad creatures together? Is it pity? Generosity? Or is it merely... smell--!

At this, Hayden goes for Byron who, having turned his back on the former, turns suddenly and half-accidentally, half-defensively directs his épée at his assailant. Hayden falls back and the table is set at an electric silence.

Fetch some water, Fletcher! Don't stand there gaping, look to it!

Byron approaches the wounded Hayden who, picking up a nearby épée, staggers to his feet.

HAYD: Keep away! I'll kill the man that comes near…

BYR: As you wish, Hayden – it's no more than a scratch in any case.

Fletcher hurries in with water and approaches Hayden.

Leave him, Fletcher, our 'gallant' requires no aid.

FLE: But milord--

BYR: I said leave him…! – Well, gentlemen, this is but half an evening – there are still opiates to be inhaled! We should leave now if we're not to be disappointed – or worse still, sober – Fletcher, my things!

He exits quickly followed slowly by others. Hayden collapses. Fletcher remains behind and goes quickly to Hayden. Through the rest of the scene, servants come and go with bowls of clean water.

HAYD: Thank you, Fletcher. Not good with the sight of blood - always makes me feel sick..

FLE: Easy does it, now, sir…

HAYD: Unromantic to the last, eh Fletcher? Help me up…

FLE: You're going nowhere, sir, rest now.

HAYD: The child, Fletcher, I must take her back to her mother. You can help me get to the convent…

FLE: Miss Allegra's not there anymore sir. She had a fever - they moved her to a peasant's place. I didn't want to leave her--

HAYD: How can you serve such a man, Fletcher?

FLE: Don't know as I can anymore. He's changed. Doesn't seem in control of hisself anymore. Begging your pardon, sir - he never could stand having old flames around once the fire's gone out. Makes him angry, and being angry makes him cruel: the more they hang on the crueller he gets.

HAYD: Then you think… Claire - Miss Claremont, I mean, still loves him?

FLE: I expect she does, sir – I mean--

HAYD: Yes, of course - I've been stupid. If I'd been more patient. I mean, she might have learned in time, to love… me - do you think…? *(for a moment pain overcomes him).*

FLE: I'm sure she would, sir…

HAYD: Instead of which…it's all come to nothing…

He dies. Fletcher lowers Hayden's gently, speaking as he does so.

FLE: *I'll* fetch the child, sir…whatever it takes.

Fade

End of Act Three.

ACT 4. Sc 1

Outside the gates of the abbey. Same time. Shelley and Trelawney are travel-worn and weary. Trelawney beats three times on door. 'C'e qualcuno?' "Is anyone there?" etc. They wait. Shelley casts a look around.

SHEL: September…. Everything's falling apart - why not one's illusions? If only we could paint our own decay as consummately as Autumn: purple on gold. But the gods gave us a darker palette, did they not? Shades of loss and separation. *(pause)* I'd like to believe Byron didn't *mean* to hurt her.

Shelley beats on the door again. A voice is heard shouting back: 'Arrivo, arrivo!

Fade.

4.2

Byron's dressing-room. Later that evening. He paces about as Fletcher hands him his accoutrements. Elise brushes her hair.

BYR: You went to get her yourself!?

FLE: *(presenting Byron with ink and paper)* The peasant woman wouldn't give her to me without your permission.

BYR: I should have you flogged! *(scrawls a note)*

FLE: You'd've fetched 'er straight away if you'd clapped eyes on that hovel!

BYR: All right, all right, for god's sake I've already told Mrs Shelley they can have the girl back!

96

FLE: They won't know where to find 'er!

BYR: Stop bleating and take this *(blots note and hands it to Fletcher)* - go back and get her, Fletcher, but for god's sake leave me alone - and don't blame me if the child takes a turn for the worse - that sin will rest with the Abbess. Take her straight to Villa Mare! God knows, if the girl needs rest she won't get it here.

FLE: No, and nor will you if I'm too late, milord.

BYR: What?

FLE: Milord.... *(with a slight bow, Fletcher exits hurriedly).*

BYR: Damn the man! Gets more insolent by the hour: if he weren't so incapable of finding another position I'd get rid of him.

ELISE: Fletcher is not so stupid as he wishes to appear.

BYR: No? And what would you know about it? God knows, I didn't rescue you from Shelley for your insight. God knows why I *did* rescue you - god knows why I've done anything in the past few weeks - I certainly don't...

Elise goes over to him but he shrugs her off.

Climate - it's all down to climate. My mind's as vague as a siesta. This heat kills thought. Then again, what's the alternative? The funereal fog of a rainy London... 'London' - the very word tolls a like a bell in one's conscience. Picture it: another season of dull aristocrats and social climbers. No, a constitution like mine needs to be constantly on the move. I need an antidote! *(suddenly animated)*

ELISE: Where are you going?

BYR: Anywhere! My only stipulation is that pleasure should be high on the menu: - transient, intense, guiltless pleasure: something I've been ignoring too much recently! Can't say when I'll be back: tonight, tomorrow, next week, next year – never!

ELISE: You're not leaving - you can't leave ---

BYR: Don't be silly, my dear – of course I can.

He turns and is instantly gone, Elise is alone.

Fade.

4.3

An inner cloister of the Abbey. Dusk that evening. Shelley and Trelawney enter urgently. At the same time Sister Francesca seeks to bar their entry. On the other side of the stage, the Abbess rises from her devotions.

Sis. F: You do not understand: these are The Mother Superior's private quarters--

SHEL: Then you may tell her I seek a private audience!

ABB: Leave us, sister, we know how little the signore respects the dignity of the Almighty – how much less that of a mere mortal. I will see just one of you.

Trelawney is waved back by Shelley. Exit Sis F.

Well, signore, what would you have us do for you?

SHEL: Nothing, Abbess. I assure you: the less you do for me the better!

98

ABB: Indeed, signore – would all ignorant men were as selfless!

SHEL: And that you were more selfish with your holy wisdom! – I've come for my niece, if you send for her I'll waste no more of your time.

ABB: Unfortunately, that I cannot do.

SHEL: Cannot or will not?

ABB: Both, as it happens. I should tell you that when he originally left his daughter in our care, milord Byron was explicit in his desire that you be prevented from seeing the child, signore. It seems he deemed your influence unsuitable with respect to her career as a Christian--

SHEL: She has no 'career' as a Christian, she's a child, damn you!

ABB: No doubt you would damn us all if you could, signore – if not with your bare hands then at least with your thoughts, no? *(she chuckles complacently to herself)*

SHEL: Please send for the child, Abbess.

ABB: But even if I had the power to return her, signore, don't you think I would be false to my faith in doing so; just as you would be true to yours in taking her? Are you really so happy to see others betray their own convictions? And then there's the child herself - of course, a child cannot truly know what belief is--

SHEL: Nor shall she be sacrificed to it in the name of her father's ignorance! Now please send for her Abbess!

ABB: But is not faith the guide of ignorance, signore? And do you think I would really hand her over to someone who sought to destroy that faith even before she had learned to build it?

SHEL: Faith? Surely fear would be a better word!

ABB: The fear of god is part of the construct of faith--

SHEL: The foundation of it, more like! How is it, Abbess, that your omnipotent god is so dependent on his followers' fear?

ABB: He is not dependent – fear is his gift to us.

SHEL: A generous god!

ABB: Without fear there would be no moral order! Man would revert to savagery…! But let us not raise our voices, signore; perhaps we have more in common than you think….What if I were to tell you that neither I myself believe in the grand old man with the grey beard floating on a cloud, what then, eh? That this is just a silly picture painted to please the childish minds of simpletons? Call him the god of fate, fortune or necessity, something that punishes and rewards - what does it matter what the common man believes so long as he accepts something higher than himself? Believe me, signore, it has always been so because it *must* be so.

SHEL: Unless men choose to rebel.

ABB: Ha! With you at the head of the mob! Forgive me for laughing, signore but with all the bloody evidence of history before you, you still imagine you can change human nature with a simple revolution--

SHEL: In men's hearts, not the streets, Abbess.

ABB: Men's hearts are weak, signore - ask Satan.

SHEL: But Satan's under god's control! – or are we worshipping the wrong man, Abbess? That is assuming, of course, we have the power to choose…

100

ABB: Free will is man's birthright--

SHEL: Then why does your god damn him for it!? Your god may be higher than those he commands, Abbess, but he's just as much a slave to his own passions - his desire to be worshipped would be pathetic if it weren't so poisonous!

ABB: How dare you speak so in the house of the Lord!

SHEL: Because I know what a weak and feeble-minded character he really is! If I deny him, Abbess, he simply disappears...

At this point Shelley casually extinguishes the candles lit beneath a crucifix. Apart from a vivid silhouette, they are plunged into near darkness. The Abbess utters stunned imprecations.

ABB: Per l'amor' di Christo! Bring light – Sister Francesca - Paola! Summon assistance!

SHEL: Are you really so afraid of the dark, Abbess?

ABB: Your words offend god--

SHEL: Would they could destroy him! But that would leave you orphaned in the face of your own fear. - Your religion, Abbess, is nothing but a child's reasoning away the hours of darkness and your god nothing but a phantasm that profits from a nightmare.

ABB: And your thoughts are filthy poisons that fill you with the pride of your own intellect and blind you to the truth! Would the stake could still purge them away!

SHEL: Ah yes – the gospel of love! -

Enter two workmen and Sisters P. and F. with lantern &
candlelight. Trelawney follows.

ABB: He has desecrated our shrine - throw the infidel out!

The men seize him.

And his mercenary with him! I would gladly light the first
flame at your pyre, and I would do it to preserve the dignity
of god – and I would do it in the knowledge that the Lord
Jesus would forgive me. Yes, signore, the same saviour that
died for our sins – even yours!

SHEL: Christ died for nothing, Abbess. *(shakes off his captors)* - I
came here for my niece: deliver her to me and I'll be gone.

The Abbess's tone is suddenly cold.

ABB: That is quite impossible.

SHEL: Then I'll fetch her myself. *(makes to go)*

ABB: Then you must take something to pay Charon with,
signore…

Shelley stops, he comprehends the significance of the
Abbess's words.

SHEL: It were better not to joke in such matters, Abbess.

ABB: No joke was implied, I assure you, signore: the girl is dead.

Shelley stares at her momentarily dumbfounded.

She was brought here in high fever. Unfortunately, there was
nothing we could do…

102

Shelley moves toward her but is restrained by the men.

Though as the good Lord is our witness, we tried! Had you listened to me when you broke in here -: I told you it no longer lay within my power to restore her to you.

SHEL: Take me to her!

ABB: She is dead, signore.

TRE: You're lying!

ABB: For once, I wish I were, signore.

SHEL: Then take me to her grave!

ABB: Where have the fever victims been buried?

Sis P: Upon the hillside; outside the cemetery, Reverend Mother...
        - but the girl--

ABB: Enough! Sisters, take these signori to the graveyard - if you value your salvation do not converse with them.

        The Abbess turns away and starts relighting the candles as Shelley and Trelawney exit with the workmen and Sister Paola. Sister Francesca lingers accusatively, sensing her presence the Abbess turns round. No sooner seeing her she turns away again.

ABB: The truth, sister..? Some do not deserve such a treasure....

        Fade.

4.4

Another - this time almost deserted - osteria. Nightfall same time as previous scene. Polidori sits idly carousing, Byron paces thoughtfully back and forth, trailing his épée over the furniture. He passes by Polidori and takes his wine glass.

BYR: Goodness... *(he drains glass and hands it back)* Good... ness. No, I wouldn't call myself a 'good' man, as such. But then what is a 'good' act but a kind of ransom to buy off one's conscience, and what is conscience but a surrender to common opinion? Being able to stand quite alone, that's the thing: we'd all be wicked if we had the nerve: sometimes I wish I had the courage to be worse - not better - than I am!

POL: Hear, hear!

BYR: Dissect the holiest action and you'll find a refined self-interest at the heart of it! Doing good by stealth? Pointless! What could be more frustrating than being kind without anyone noticing it! No, vanity dictates that we must be *seen* to be good: - and if, for some miserable reason, folk should miss our splendid moral show, we can always review it in private: a good bit of self-congratulation does wonders for the heart! What do you think, Polly? For instance, have I been a 'good' friend?

POLI: Can't remember.

BYR: All right – a good father, then?

Polidori splutters into his wine.

POLI: You mean, you *have* off-spring?

BYR: So they tell me, Polly, so they tell me... *(he turns away)* If I had to fight a duel with Shelley, who d'yer think'd win? I mean - it'd be a shame to hurt him: after all, when all is said and done, he's the closest thing I've ever had to a friend.

POLI: Oh, boo hoo...!

BYR: Not that friendship really exists, as such: when it comes down to it, I've always thought man's natural state was war: what we call friendship is merely an uneasy truce that serves both sides.

Polidori snores audibly. Byron picks up his épée casually.

Polly, has anyone ever told you what a worthless sot you are?

POLI: No.

He swigs from his wine glass, Byron hits it away with the épée.

BYR: Then let me be the first.

POLI: What in hell's name...

BYR: Time you left, Polly.

POLI: What *are* you talking about!

BYR: Time! *(presses his épée into Polidori)*

POLI: What?

BYR: To depart, decamp - dis...appear...

POLI: Have you gone finally mad?

105

BYR: No, I've gone finally sane, now get out! Here's the only thing you've ever loved! *(Byron throws money at Polidori)* If I find you in this country after supper I'm quite liable… *(flicking the épée across Polidori's hand, scratching it)* – to kill you.

Uttering a cry of pain, Polidori staggers backwards in disbelief. The two stand staring at each other, Byron raising an eyebrow in ironic contempt. Polidori registers Byron's resolve and exits.

4.5

A cemetery near the Abbey. Same time. Shelley and Trelawney, holding lanterns, are led by the two nuns, Sisters Paola and Francesca, to a child's grave. One of them points to one in particular.

SHEL: Why is there no name? No flowers..?

TRE: Shelley--

SHEL: This is unconsecrated ground. *(to Sis. P)* How is this so?

Sis P: Signore?

SHEL: Is it the Abbess's practice to consign children that die in her care to anonymous graves?

Sis. P: The child, signore…The Reverend Mother was not sure if baptism ---

SHEL: To hell with baptism! *(he seizes Sister Paola's arm)* Why is the grave unmarked?

TRE: Shelley--!

SHEL: Answer me!

Sis. F: A headstone would not stand in the earth yet, signore - when
           it has settled--

SHEL: It never shall…. *(silence)* What have I done? *(he starts
           distractedly placing stones as a border round the grave.*

TRE: This is Byron's doing…you trusted him - he gave his word!

SHEL: And I was naive enough to accept it! *(suddenly he starts to
           dig with bare hands at the grave.)* I've got to see her! -
           What if this isn't her? What if there's been some mistake ---

TRE: Shelley, for god's sake!

SHEL: How can I go back to Clare with this? Bare earth and stones?

TRE: You did what you thought best for her. – What will you do,
           go back with a body?!

           *He grasps Shelley and pulls him to his feet, Shelley resists:
           in a fit of angst he struggles with Trelawney until he comes
           to rest. They kneel to restore the earth and stones.*

           Byron wasn't fit to be a father.

SHEL: I'm going up there: I'll make him see what he's done.

TRE: Let me go to Claire. At least let me prepare her!

SHEL: How am I to tell her? What am I to say..?

           Trelawney moves away leaving Shelley kneeling.

           Fade.

4.6

The Abbess's cell. Midnight. Enter the Abbess angrily, with the two nuns, Sisters Francesca and Paola, in attendance.

ABB: Taken?!

Sis. F: The servant – Fletcher – he came after the other two left, Reverend Mother: he gave Signora Rosetta a note from Milord himself—she gave signorina Allegra over to him.

Sis. P: We thought it was enough, Mother Abbess--

ABB: God preserve us, don't you see what I'm trying to do?! That infidel family is poison! Milord Byron understood that. He was happy for us to bring his daughter to God. Now the bastard child will be restored to her whore of a mother. Listen to me! What do you see when you look at that Englishman – that infidel? Just a romantic young man, eh? A poet!

Sis. F: Yes, a poet - no-one pays them any attention any more.

ABB: Fool! What chance do you think we have with such naivety as our only defence!

Sis. F: Reverend Mother?

ABB: It is not only poetry that is a thing of the past, sister! It is us! The church! That man, sisters - that godless young fool: he is the future, don't you see? *(silence)* You don't see anything….

the nuns shift uneasily.

It is passing, sisters… so quickly…. *(goes to window)*. The great age of belief, of order. One day you will look out over

108

this landscape and there will be no sound of distant bells in the valleys, no visitors at our gates…. The churches will be empty… - Chiese deserte, abandonnate….Yes! Another century perhaps - not more. Another hundred autumns! I have seen thirty myself from this very window! It has always been my favourite view: the cemetery, the cypresses - gli alberi dei morti…trees of the dead. *(silence, then a bell begins to toll)* - What is the hour?

Sis. F: Towards midnight, Reverend Mother.

ABB: Already? - Give me your arm, sister - or I shall never get up for Dawn Prayer.

Sis. P: You are tired, Reverend Mother.

ABB: No, sister, I am not tired…. I am old.

Exit. Slow fade…

4.7

Villa Mare. Same time. Enter Mary and Claire. They are highly animated. Claire seems unwilling to enter the room, and is almost led by the arm by Mary.

CLA: I must stay with her!

MARY: Let her sleep. She'll be all right now – I promise you!

CLA: But--

MARY: She's in the next room - nobody can get to her. *(she clasps Claire's hands and looks her full in the face)* - Allegra's back with us – forever…

Claire returns Mary's gaze then embraces her in a mixture of tears and laughter. Enter Trelawney and Fletcher.

FLE: Like some witch, she was, preying on the child with her potions.

MARY: Fletcher, Shelley knows nothing of your master's change of heart about Allegra: you must reach them before anything happens!

FLE: I'll fetch the horses...

Exit Fletcher. Claire turns to go back to Allegra's room. Mary gently intercepts her.

MARY: Let me sit with her, dearest, if it makes you feel better. You should rest.

Exit Mary, leaving Trelawney and Claire facing each other ruefully.

TRE: Thank god for Fletcher!

They both laugh. Then silence.

CLA: I'll never forgive him. I'll never let him see her again - never.

Pause. Suddenly Claire fulminates.

How could he do it? Send his own child away like that! His own flesh and blood! *(pause)* - Why did we think it would work? This absurd arrangement? *(wearily)* Paradise on earth!

TRE: We forgot to leave the snake behind.

CLA: I can't stay here. We have to leave.

110

TRE: We *will* leave.

CLA: Tomorrow! *(she sees Trelawney's rueful glance)* Well - as soon as possible - as far away as possible. I don't care where! We could go together!

TRE: *(smiling)* I hear Russia's not without its attractions…

CLA: Yes! Moscow! We'll wear great fur-coats and drink vodka in the snow!

TRE: And wake up with heads as sore as bears!

CLA: And won't remember anything that's happened!

TRE: Yes, we'll forget everything!

Claire laughs and takes Trelawney's hands.

CLA: Yes! - where we come from - where we're going - who we are…

TRE: We'll forget ourselves entirely!

CLA: And everything'll be all right!

Suddenly they kiss. Enter Fletcher.

FLE: Everything's ready, Master Trelawney, we should go - for Master Shelley's sake!

Recovering his sense of urgency, Trelawney takes his riding crop from Fletcher.

CLA: Quickly – go!

Trelawney glances back at her as he & Fletcher exit. Fade.

4.8

Byron's drawing-room. After midnight. Shelley is seated in shadow. In a distant corridor a song begins to make itself heard. As it becomes louder the door opens and in saunters Byron. He is unsober but not drunk, and casually carrying two épées, one over each shoulder. He continues singing, oblivious of Shelley's presence.

'So she led me to a secret dell,
Where midnight flowers bloom
Where only gentle creatures dwell,
And the serpent finds no room...'

Never could sing... who cares!

'If you say no when your heart says yes,
You never shall find your true love,
Never say no when you know you mean yes,
Lest your lie wake the moon above...'

He pours himself a glass of wine, turns to sit down, and sees Shelley.

BYR: Shelley, my dear fellow... *(throws an épée in seat next to door)*

SHEL: I let myself in.

BYR: So I see, so I see! Well, you find me—

SHEL: Singing.

BYR: If you can call it that! - A mournful tune: one that goes with your expression, if I may say so. I must've known you were coming.

SHEL: And I should've known you were lying.

BYR: Oh Shel, must we pursue this - posturing in private? Of course, I understand why in front of the others…where are they, by the way? I was expecting some form of deputation… if only to thank me…

Shelley looks incredulously at him.

Still - if we're to be alone - well, nearly alone: the fiery Elise is bowling around somewhere. *(in a sing-song voice)* "I can seeeeee yoooou….!" *(he turns conspiratorially to Shelley)* She tried to bite me the other day! Or was it I who tried to bite her? Anyway! She has express orders never to enter this room! We may speak in utter confidence…

SHEL: She's dead, Byron.

BYR: What…? –

SHEL: Your daughter.

BYR: What are you talking about?

SHEL: Allegra. At the convent. Where you abandoned her…ill – alone…

BYR: Is this some species of joke, Shelley?

Shelley stares at him impassively. Byron's expression darkens. When? How - how did it happen?

SHEL: A few hours ago, typhus…

BYR: -- But Fletcher went to--! - I told Mary - the Abbess assured me --- ! Why was I not informed? They said it wasn't serious.

113

SHEL: Then you knew--?

BYR: They said they'd keep me advised--

SHEL: Of what: your duty as a father? A human being?

Byron demurs, his rage barely suppressed.

BYR: I told them: she was to have everything! I said: spare no expense. And anyway, I wrote a damned letter to bring her home--

SHEL: For God's sake, stop lying! You're the worst kind of coward, Byron: you're a disease: you infect everyone who touches you - even your own daughter! Well, now she's dead. I had hoped you might have the guts to console her mother...

So saying, Shelley makes to exit but Byron moves across to lean against the door blocking his path.

Let me pass.

BYR: I did what I could for the child! You've hounded me - as good as blackmailed me - ever since the poor creature's mother conceived her! God knows, there are those who think me mad for indulging you as much as I have! After all, there's no proof who the child's real father is, is there?

Shelley suppresses his anger.

Oh don't look so shocked: you know the rumours as well as I do - a pair of sisters all over you - not that I blame you for that: you are, despite what you like to think - only human. But the fact remains that, with your little 'ménage', some might say you out-did me in the provision of your own... comforts..

Shelley, still refusing to surrender to Byron's anger, makes to open the door again, but Byron bars the way by placing his épée between Shelley's chin and the door. Shelley pushes away the épée slowly, but as he does so Byron pulls it cutting Shelley. Shelley finally picks up the other épée in fury and they fight. Both sustain light wounds.

BYR: *(out of breath)* There, you do have a temper – just a little slow off the mark, that's all – nothing like a bit of violence to quicken the blood…

Shelley pushes Byron backwards and throws down his own épée. At this point enter a drunken Elise carrying a wine bottle. She picks up the épée and mocks both of them.

ELISE: Ah, little boys with their swords – is it over me?

BYR: Hardly, my dear – fetch us some water.

ELISE: Fetch it yourself – *(she throws wine over him)* – You thought I'd just retire gracefully – like one of your well-bred English ladies! *(as she passes he wrests the bottle from her)*

BYR: Who could possibly confuse you with one of them!

ELISE: Thought I'd just take my place in your list of conquests--

BYR: You should be grateful I count you amongst them - god knows, you were scarcely memorable! Now give me that toy sword…

As he nonchalantly puts down the wine bottle on a table and turns round to take the épée from her, but with a sudden, clinical, eerie calmness, she seriously wounds him. As he looks at his own blood on his hand, Fletcher and Trelawney enter. She pushes past them. Shelley goes to Byron's aid.

115

SHEL: Leave her, give me some water!

Fletcher does so.

BYR: Yes, yes, a spot of blood, Fletcher – don't make a fuss;
        we've had enough hysteria for one day.

*Fletcher helps Byron to a chaise. Trelawney offers his help
to Shelley who, more concerned with Byron, declines it.*

SHEL: Had to play the fool…

BYR: I do it so well, Shelley - and one should never waste talent.

TRE: Your daughter's alive, Byron! *(he casts a glance at Shelley
        who is amazed).*

FLE: I took her from the peasant woman, milord - she's back with
        her mother - she's that much better, sir, the fever's passing.

BYR: Remind me to speak to you about your sense of timing,
        Fletcher.

TRE: *(to Shelley)* The Abbess *was* lying – it wasn't Allegra's
        grave.

BYR: Never trust women of the cloth, Shelley - they're all odd.
        Damned woman…wanted to come swimming with me….
        (beat) Help me up, Fletcher, I should like to go and see my
        daughter.

All three men remonstrate.

SHEL: You can see her later.

BYR: Yes, no doubt it is a bit late. Cooler tonight, summer's over
        thank Christ – a relief from all that bloody heat! You know

116

[Byron cont.]

why midnight's the most peaceful time of day? Because it's too late to change anything…

He tries to rise again and just manages to stand - furiously gesturing the men away -

I wish to see my daughter! I need a favour from her - undeserved, maybe, but then, for a Byron, she has a most forgiving nature –

He is failing again and Fletcher approaches to lower him to the ground –

- something she did not learn…from her father. *(dies)*

FLE: *(kneels by Byron)* Milord?

SHEL: Fetch water! Salts - *(starts hunting around himself but hasn't the strength to continue).* A surgeon - Trelawney!

TRE: *(grasps Shelley)* Shelley – it's too late.

Trelawney lets a disbelieving Shelley go, the two men stand in silence.

Fade.

4.9

Villa Mare. A week later. Bright late afternoon sunlight. Claire stands alone by the window. Enter Fletcher with a tray of wine and glasses which he puts down.

FLE: Beautiful out today, ma'am.

CLA: *(distracted)* Mm?

FLE: Lovely sunlight! - the sea all glittering and that... I mean, if you like that kind of thing ---

CLA: I think poets are wrong about nature - she's heartless. All she cares about is her own beauty – however miserable we mortals are....

FLE: Ah well, you may have something there.

         Silence.

CLA: Allegra looks so like him, don't you think..?

FLE: Ah those eyes, miss! Couldn't mistake them, that's for sure!

CLA: She would've been proud of her father...*(she turns away in tears, Fletcher stands by in silence, as she recovers)* Some say the soul experiences great bliss at the moment of death: – that suddenly, on being freed from the body the spirit can go anywhere it wants - in time or space - relive any memory just by thinking... just by thinking.

         Silence.

         What will you do, Fletcher?

FLE: Ma'am?

CLA: I know there isn't much to keep you here...

         A child's laughter sounds, then Mary's voice calling

         "Allegra!"

FLE: More than enough, ma'am...

118

Enter Mary with Trelawney. She is calling for Allegra.

MARY: Allegra?! - Oh, I'm sorry--

CLA: It's all right.

MARY: I could've sworn she was in here. This house plays tricks with voices. Have you seen Shelley? He said he was going out in the boat - but there's a storm coming...

FLE: That won't stop Master Shelley...

TRE: It'll only encourage him! But I'll give him a shout for you...

He exits.

MARY: And Allegra! She might come if *you* call her. Claire?

CLA: She can have one last play while we walk along the beach...!

They exit, leaving Fletcher polishing a wine glass, he breathes on it, polishes it again; then, as he holds it up to the light -

Fade.

End.

Poets

James Murphy
© 2018
The Heretic's Press

ISBN 978-1-9996149-1-1
www.hereticspress.co.uk
contact: info@hereticspress.co.uk

www.ingramcontent.com/pod-product-compliance
Lightning Source LLC
Chambersburg PA
CBHW031516040426
42445CB00009B/255